GLORY GUNNERS

Think Portsm

Think footb

Think Fratton ....

Think again...

A century has passed since the demise of the best football club Portsmouth has ever seen. The vanished decades have hidden the achievements of the Royal Artillery FC. They were an elite service outfit which swept all before them in an unsurpassed five year period. They made the national headlines during their rapid ascent as they won cup competitions against opponents from around the country. They made headlines again, for the wrong reasons, as their fortunes were wrecked in an instant in a payment scandal which reached the very top of the footballing establishment.

Never far from controversy, RA's goalkeeper Matt Reilly symbolised the club's two sides. He was Portsmouth's first sporting star. Brilliant enough to be capped for his country he was courted by the top clubs of his day. He was idolised by the thousands of fans who packed The Gunners' home games in the heart of the city to create the biggest sporting spectacles it had known. But he was also familiar to officialdom's disciplinarians for the less acceptable aspects of his game. His role in RA's history has stayed buried in the archives since Victorian times. The club's legacies, however, have continued to shape football in Portsmouth even as it prepares to enter the new millennium.

The inheritance they bequeathed to soccer in the city included the very words – Play up Pompey – at the heart of every true Pompey fan. This book brings to life the story behind the men who paved the way for professional football in Portsmouth.

KEVIN SMITH

Acknowledgements

Researching this book would have been impossible without the extensive help provided by Carol Farr, the librarian at The News Centre in Portsmouth.

I am also grateful for the assistance over several years of the librarians on the second floor reference section at Portsmouth's Central Library.

More specific help has been given by: Mick Cooper, Allan Craven, Anne-Marie Maguire, Keith Newbery and Tony Valvona with their comments about the final form of this book; Mick Cooper and Tony Valvona have also allowed me access to their collections of football memorabilia; Ben Stoneham, the managing director of Portsmouth Printing & Publishing Ltd, with permission to reproduce the company's material; David Barber, of the FA; Brian Fellows, with permission to use his research into the origins of the Pompey Chimes; Major Terry Knight, of the Army FA; Mona Abbott and Jill King, Portsmouth Tourist Guides Association; and Carl Allen, Harwich and Parkeston FC historian.

My thanks also go to the many colleagues within Portsmouth Publishing & Printing Ltd – such as Pat Argent, Eileen Kemp and Rosemary Phillips – who have helped with my efforts on the Glory Gunners.

My principal reference sources have been the *Portsmouth Evening News*, the *Hampshire Telegraph*, the *Southern Daily Mail* and the *Portsmouth Times*.

Additional information has been gathered from:
Pompey - the history of Portsmouth Football Club;
Hampshire League - A Tabulated League History;
75 Years of Southern League Football;
The Times Illustrated History of Football;
Caxton's Association Football.

GLORY GUNNERS

GLORY GUNNERS

The history of the
Royal Artillery (Portsmouth) F.C.

KEVIN SMITH

KS PUBLICATIONS 1999

First published in 1999 by Kevin Smith
c/o 14 Station Road,. Bognor Regis, West Sussex P021 IQE

© 1999 Kevin Smith
All rights reserved.

Produced by Woodfield Publishing Services
(book and journal printing specialists), Bognor Regis, West Sussex.

ISBN 0 9534707 0 9

*Bombardier John Hanna, RA's captain and centre-forward
and the first international footballer in Portsmouth.*

Contents

"What may be the future of the Royal Artillery it is hard to say. The probabilities are that next year will see them forced into a "back seat" role by the new Portsmouth professional team, and engaging only in the Army Cup and such-like mild diversions. They will not be forgotten, however, as a unique Army team, a collection of brilliant players. Reilly is one of the best goalkeepers in the world and Hanna was honoured with a place in the Irish international team versus Wales on March 4. And as the club which made the association game in Portsmouth."

Portsmouth Evening News, April 29, 1899

The Chimes – The Origins

Play up Pompey! Pompey play up!

Six words which are famous throughout the footballing world – and they owe everything to Royal Artillery. The 'Glory Gunners' were the inspiration for the Pompey Chimes which create passion among the players who wear the blue shirts, loyalty among their fans and a mixture of fear and admiration in their opponents. The chant is likely to be the oldest football anthem in the country, if not in the soccer-playing world.

It is fitting the rhyme's origins lie with Royal Artillery. For the club gave winning, organised football to Portsmouth and sowed a legacy of success a century ago.

The potency of the Pompey label was still as strong as ever as 1999 began. A centenary exhibition held to mark the present professional club's past was called 'Play up Pompey'. The display was staged at the Portsmouth City Museum, itself with strong links to RA in its former guise of Clarence Barracks for having housed some of the army team's players.

Proof of the Pompey connection with the Artillerymen is provided by the Harwich and Dovercourt Free Press on February 25, 1899, on the day of one of RA's biggest matches, and certainly their most fateful. The newspaper stated that The Gunners were 'known in their neighbourhood as Pompey'.

That mention shows how the nickname had already become well established with the exploits of the Artillerymen and, like most matters Pompey, illustrates how the current club is following the path set down by the military side. It was to be a further seven months after that Harwich newspaper report before the professional club's players took part in their first competitive game.

The nickname has become so powerful and all-pervading it has gained entries in the latest editions of at least two authoritative reference books, including the *Oxford Dictionary of Slang*, published in 1998, for being used to refer to the whole city as well as to its football club.*

*The term's date of origin is given as 1899 to strengthen its connection with RA.

A possible explanation of the distinctive name's link with The Gunners has come from City of Portsmouth guide Peter Saunders. He told *The News* (Portsmouth) that thousands of soldiers in Portsmouth annually paraded in Victorian times for the monarch's birthday.

But RA were ordered to line the route one year instead of marching. They protested that the job was not one for a senior regiment in the British Army, being suited in the Bastille Day parade in Paris to the fire brigade. The next time the RA team took to the field it was to the teasing cry of "Here come the Pompiers", after the French name for firemen. The name quickly became adapted to Pompey and was acquired by the current Portsmouth FC after RA's demise.

Other explanations for the origins of Pompey lie with the 80-gun French warship *Le Pompee*, which was captured in 1793, and became the guardship of Portsmouth Harbour when Britain and France were at war, and the exploits of a group of sailors who climbed Pompey's Pillar near Alexandria in Egypt in 1781 to become "Pompey's Boys".

What the paper's say

'Huddersfield were swamped by the sheer passion and desire of Ball's players – and the deafening sound of the Pompey Chimes.'
The Sun

John Westwood leads the fans with bugle and bell

'If ever a crowd has kept a club afloat, it is Alan Ball's self-styled "Blue and White Army".'
The Times

The Pompey Chimes, still making the news in 1998 – more than a hundred years after they were first sung.

But RA's bequeathing of the Chimes lies in a geographic coincidence right in the heart of Portsmouth. It was in 1890 that the roots of the link between Pompey the nickname and the simple, but effective anthem began. In that year the original Portsmouth Town Hall was completed. A chiming turret clock was installed in the building and began to sound out when the civic centrepiece was opened by the then Prince of Wales.

Its chimes could clearly be heard a few years later when RA's successes began to attract crowds of 2,000 and upwards to its Burnaby Road ground within the United Services' complex a short walk away.

Evidence that The Gunners' supporters were the forerunners of the Fratton End fans and used to sing along in unison, and possible imitation of the clock, can be found in a letter written to the Football Mail as memories were stirred by the current club's golden jubilee.

Portsmouth were at the peak of their league form and the Chimes boomed out from a packed Fratton Park every home game when "Follower" from County Down put pen to paper in January 1949. Just over 50 years earlier the scene, if not the location, was much the same.

He told of attending his first football match on October 9, 1897, and hearing the vocal efforts of the crowd standing ten-deep behind Matt Reilly's goal. "Follower" was 16 and serving in the navy. He went with a friend in the training brig HMS Sealark to watch RA at the US Ground where the goals had no nets and the rope-lined pitch ran parallel to the railway line. The admission was 2d:

'The town hall clock chimed the quarter hours and in those days the referees relied on the clock for the time the game should last. Full time was at 4 o'clock and at two or three minutes to four RA

were leading, but hard pressed, so the crowd at Reilly's goal kept lilting in unison with the chimes of the hour, apparently with the idea of reminding the referee to blow his whistle for full time.'

Further proof of the origin of the Chimes came from a fellow RA supporter. Using the pen name "No Fan", he wrote to the *Football Mail* about watching The Gunners in the mid-1890s:

'My recollection is that the RA goalkeeper was 6ft-plus and named Reilly, who later became Pompey's first goalkeeper and was promptly nicknamed Town Hall, the Portsmouth Town Hall then being a comparatively new building and by far the tallest in the town. I believe he was encouraged by calls of "Well Done Town Hall", and the Chimes soon followed to be carried all over the world in His Majesty's ships.'

The first mention of the Chimes in a newspaper report backs "No Fan's" memory, though it appeared several years after the game he recalled. *The Portsmouth Evening News* journalist at one of Pompey's early Southern League home fixtures – against Brighton United on September 23, 1899 – described the sound as the Town Hall Chimes rang out.

He wrote that the stands and banks of the ground were packed for the game with 9,000 fans:

'Spectators gave the visitors their first taste of the Town Hall Chimes after Portsmouth had gone 1–0 up after two minutes thanks to an A. Brown shot.'

The Chimes were also featured again when the lead was doubled just before half-time.

It would have been natural for The Gunners' fans, after their team's forced disbandment in 1899, to transfer their allegiance a mile or so away to Fratton Park to enable them to continue watching top quality football.

Another RA fan also linked the town hall with the Chimes, though Mr E. L. Lloyd, of Cowler Avenue, put the start of the distinctive rhyme firmly at the time of

'Passionate about Pompey' sums up the supporters in the Fratton End (UJC Stand) – the successors to RA's home end fans.

Pompey's first game at Fratton Park in September 1899. More exactly, he said it stemmed from the time of Pompey's first competitive goal at the new ground when they took on Reading in the Southern League:

'At the precise moment when they scored the goal,' said Mr Lloyd, 'the town hall clock boomed forth and supporters took up the refrain with Hullo, Hullo, Hullo, Hullo.'

But his account would seem to be disproved by the fact Clarke scored the goal 20 minutes after the kick-off. The second goal, by Whittaker, offers no joy either, being scored after 48 minutes. Neither time would have matched the clock chiming.

Indeed, the match report only noted 'deafening cheers arose' after Whittaker's goal. Even that description of the reaction was rare. Reports of RA's games hardly ever ventured away from straight ball-by-ball descriptions.

But the *Portsmouth Evening News'* journalists at the new club's early competitive matches soon began to vary the style as the season got underway. The chant's name quickly evolved. The Town Hall Chimes description of the October 28 match with Swindon Town was replaced within a month by the mention of simply The Chimes when Bristol City were the opponents on November 25.

Within a further two weeks, they had been given their current title of the Pompey Chimes. But that occasion was in connection with events off the pitch. A Mr John Tonks took the chant from the terraces to the courtroom after he was charged with using obscene language at 1 a.m. in Commercial Road.

One of the several witnesses who were called said Tonks (23) and others were only singing the Pompey Chimes. Not for the last time, the legal personnel were clueless about popular culture. The witness gave an impromptu demonstration to the magistrates by singing "Hallo! Hallo!" amid much laughter in the court. Tonks, however, had little to laugh about. He was still convicted of the charge and fined 4s 6d plus 10s 6d costs.

The closest guide to the original words of the Chimes can be found in the 1900/01 official handbook of Portsmouth FC: 'Play up Pompey. Just one more goal! Make tracks! What ho! Hallo! Hallo!'

The passing of the decades has seen the words of the Chimes modified along with the tune. The present rendering is a slightly simplified version of the Westminster chimes, which ring out of the Portsmouth Guildhall clock. The potency of the anthem is as strong as ever, though, as Portsmouth FC passed their 100th birthday in April 1998.

Football magazine *Four Four Two* used the headline 'Play Up Pompey, Pompey Play Up' when it featured an article about naval football that month, and Fratton Park's social venue is called The Pompey Chimes. Manager Alan Ball evoked the Chimes a few months earlier in his first home programme notes of his second spell at the club. He wrote:

'I am sure you will all get right behind us this afternoon and give the team very positive support with those famous Pompey Chimes ringing out loud and clear.'

The Sun newspaper took up the theme when it reported on Portsmouth FC's narrow escape from relegation in the Nationwide League division one in 1997/98:

'Huddersfield were swamped by the sheer passion of Ball's players and the deafening sound of the Pompey Chimes. In fact, you could have floated an Isle of Wight ferry on the wave of emotion coming from them.'

So it continued as Portsmouth FC began their 100th season. Their centenary campaign opened with a pre-season tournament of friendlies launched with a rendition of the Chimes from the crowd. And the sound is joined by another surviving reminder of RA for late 20th Century football supporters around the city.

· C H A P T E R   T W O ·

Saturday Specials

T he Saturday evening read for thousands of football fans and other sporting enthusiasts in the Portsmouth area is the most visible of RA's enduring' influences on the game. The weekly newspaper, the *Sports Mail*, owes its existence to the burgeoning interest caused by The Gunners' rising fortunes a century ago. The existing newspapers – three were competing for readers in Portsmouth at the time – could not devote the space necessary to cater for the rising demand for information. So the *Southern Daily Mail* decided on an 'extraordinary departure in local journalism', as it called the move in September 1898.

That development was the publication of an edition on Saturday evenings devoted to sport, principally the latest developments which concerned RA. The new newspaper was a broadsheet printed on coloured paper every Saturday from September 17 – just before RA faced Reading in their first home match in the Southern League first division.

The Football Mail was launched to build on the Saturday afternoon football editions of the *Southern Daily Mail* which had achieved sales of 5,000 copies. Initial details of the special evening edition were revealed on September 8:

'Owing to the great success with which the football edition of the Southern Daily Mail *has met in former years, it has been decided during the season which has just commenced to publish an entirely new and separate paper which will be known as the* Football Mail.'

The features which had made the football edition so popular, such as the Ball by Ball gossip column and the grand skill competition, with a newly increased £10 first prize, would be supplemented by extra articles about football and sport in general, the proud editor announced:

'It will cater not only for the lover of football but… for all who take an interest in sport of any kind. It will be published at the same time as the old football edition but will be printed on buff paper to distinguish it from other editions of the paper.'

Four days later, and the locally ground-breaking impact of the new venture was spelt out in greater detail by the *Southern Daily Mail* to leave its readers in no doubt about how big a development they were about to witness:

'The success which has attended the football edition of the Southern Daily Mail *in past years has encouraged the proprietors to make an extraordinary departure in local journalism. This is nothing more or less than the issuing each Saturday of an* entirely new publication *dealing exclusively with football and other sports. The great growth of the game in this district has made it impossible for us to deal at length with the winter pastime without encroaching on the other columns of the paper. This has made the publication of a sporting paper proper and necessary.'*

It would also deal with the complaints from non-sports lovers that football was keeping out general news from the newspaper's usual Saturday editions.

The *Football Mail* had a lot to live up to. And it did, at least according to the newspaper's comments. "*Football Mail* an instantaneous success", boasted the *Southern Daily Mail* of October 22, along with the advertisement – "*Football Mail* every Saturday night."

Unfortunately, no initial copies of the ground-breaking publication seem to have lasted the decades. But enough information remains about the *Southern Daily Mail*'s previous soccer reporting to know that its Saturday football edition had carved out a good following in RA's early years.

The newspaper at one time felt able to boast:

'It is generally admitted that the Mail has done much to popularise our great winter pastime in Portsmouth… The Mail has always led the way in football journalism in Portsmouth, and we mean going several steps further ahead.'

The pattern was set when a match report of the club's first game – against Portsmouth Grammar School on October 6, 1894 – appeared in the 7 p.m. special edition that day.

From then on, RA and the *Southern Daily Mail*'s football coverage grew in tandem as The Gunners' fans followed the team's rapid progress to the finals of the Amateur, Hampshire and Portsmouth cups the following season.

Cahill (2) and Warrod scored for the Connaught Rangers, and Lever and Dennison for the Cameronians.

ROYAL ARTILLERY V. GRAMMAR SCHOOL.—This match was brought off this afternoon on the United Service (Men's) Ground. During the first half both teams played well, neither showing any superiority over the other. On the change of ends, however, the regiment asserted themselves, and Williams quickly scored a goal, which was followed soon after by another from Hill. The Artillery thus won by two goals to nil. Teams :—

Royal Artillery.—Riley, goal. Phillips and Williams, backs. Sergeant Roberts, Patterson, and Hill, half-backs. Robertson and Howe, right wing. Sergeant Williams, centre. Sampson and Pugh, left wing.

Grammar School.—Hickson, goal. Reed and Street, backs. Shutte, Pinnock, and Iles, half-backs. McPherson and Partridge, right wing. Woods, centre. Sheppard and Middlemas, left wing.

HARLEQUINS V. SPARTANS.—In this match, played on the Stamshaw Ground this afternoon, the Harlequins won by two goals to one. In the first half the score was level, Foot, for the Spartans, and Murray, for the Harlequins, making one each ; in the second half Knight added the winning shot. Teams :—

Harlequins.—Goal, Pearce ; backs, Elliott and Marshall ; half-backs, Norris, Gibson, and Arnold ; forwards, right wing, Thomas and Knight ; centre, Clay ; left wing, Cole and Murray.

Spartans.—Goal, H. Edwards ; backs, W. Jackson and W. Edwards; half-backs, Thorn, Garrett, and Abbott ; forwards, right wing, Masson and Clarke ; centre, Tipper ; left wing, Foot and Thorn.

PROGRESSIVES V. UNITED VICTORIAS 2ND XI.—On the Stamshaw Ground this afternoon the Progressives proved victorious by three goals to one. Davis proved of great service at back to the winners, for whom Foster scored in the first-half, the other two goals being added by Trevana in the second half. Turner scored for the losers. Teams :—

Progressive—Goal, Bankhead. Backs, Davis and Thompson. Half-backs, Barnes, Lillywhite, and Denham. Forwards : Right wing, Parkinson and Trevana. Centre, Main. Left wing, Holmes and Foster.

Victorias—Goal, Starkey. Backs, Rees and Sparrow. Half-backs, Hankins, Bagley, and Lovett. Forwards : Right wing, Newman and

The only Association match of any importance in Portsmouth was between the Cameronians and the Southsea Rovers. The soldiers' defence was exceedingly weak, and it is not suprising that they were beaten by five goals to nil. But, admitting this, it was a very good performance by the Rovers.

It is suggested by an old player of great experience that it would be a good thing if the footballers of Portsmouth were to meet to discuss points of play and law. Some time ago an international player delivered lectures on "Football, and How to Play It," in the North of England, and drew crowded houses, but it may be doubted whether football discussions would prove much of an attraction in Portsmouth. No doubt they would be useful and instructive if the youngsters of the right sort went to them, but they would probably resolve into meetings of old hands who know every move on the board, and are up to every quibble of law and case.

The statement that the Depot R.A. will have no team this year is borne out by the fact that last season's finalists have not entered for the Army Cup. Several of the men have been drafted away, but one or two at least will be found playing for other teams in the district. This will be the case with R.A. (Portsmouth) representing the gunners in Cambridge Barracks.

Several clubs are understood to object to the new rule which directs that 1s. shall be deposited with the ground man at Stamshaw on the Wednesday preceding the Saturday on which a ground has been allotted to any club. The shilling is a "guarantee of good faith" that the club will keep their engagement, and not cause any amount of trouble by having the ground marked out and then failing to turn up. The Parks and Open Spaces Committee have had to refuse a third of the applications for grounds made to them, and it is only reasonable they should take some steps to ensure that if clubs can't use their space they shall give timely notice, and thus allow another club, which may be groundless, to take their place. The real objection is that the shilling "comes not back again." Well, it is only about a halfpenny each for the twenty-two players in the match, and that cannot be called very dear for the privilege of making private for a whole afternoon a slice of a public recreation ground.

The Portsmouth R.F.C. open with a practice match to-day, and next Saturday play West London. The club will be, if anything, stronger than last year. Edmunds, after all, is not going to carry out his threat of retirement, and will

That 1895/96 season was the first in which the football edition had become a distinct entity of the *Southern Daily Mail*. In February 1896, the newspaper could boast it was the only such edition around Portsmouth, while RA's Hampshire Senior Cup semi-final with Freemantle saw sales touch 5,000.

A month later, the *Southern Daily Mail* continued its locally pioneering approach to soccer coverage as it took football on to the front page of local newspapers in Portsmouth for the first time. The extent of the importance this gave to RA's influence on the town can be gauged from the fashion of Victorian newspapers to cover their front pages with adverts.

The *Southern Daily Mail* saved space for one sentence in capitals of news just below its masthead. On March 18, it read: *'Hard lines for RA better luck on Sat'* after The Gunners' Army Cup semi-final defeat by the Royal Scots Fusiliers and the start of the build-up to the same stage in the Amateur Cup against Shrewsbury.

The front page on the eve of the Amateur Cup final on March 28 stated: *'Good luck to the RA in the Amateur Cup Final tomorrow'*

The next season, 1896/97, found the journalists seeking to aspire to greater heights in competition to the efforts of the *Portsmouth Evening News'* own football edition on Saturday evenings as RA made their debut in the Hampshire Senior League. The *Southern Daily Mail* of September 18 trumpeted the appearance of its improved football edition a week before The Gunners took on Andover in their league opener:

> *The enormous amount of time saved by the transmission of results on our Private Telegraph Wire will enable us to go to press with all the important results much earlier than was the case last season. Many new and improved features will be introduced in the football edition in the course of the season, while all the popular items of last year will be continued. "On the Ball", the popular notes of "A.N. Other", will be resumed and the doings of all local clubs chronicled. All together, we shall endeavour to maintain the reputation of the* Football Mail *for being the best football edition of any paper in the South of England.'*

Every football match played within the borough of Portsmouth would have its result included, the editor boasted, while reports of all the major games would also find a space among the comprehensive coverage. The edition's appeal to readers was summed up as follows:

> *'You must get the* Football Mail *if you want to have all the best results, read the best reports and lots of interesting gossip concerning local clubs and players'*

1897/98 saw the *Football Mail*, as the football edition came to be called even before its appearance as a separate entity, boasted of as "the smartest, brightest, most complete Football Edition out of London". The *Southern Daily Mail* sought to back up that statement by claiming:

> *'We were the first to publish such an edition in Portsmouth, and with the unique advantages placed at our disposal for the obtaining of results with the least possible delay, the* Mail *has always maintained that lead. During the coming winter no pains will be spared to make the Saturday evening edition as successful as it has been in the past.'*

On October 9, the trumpeting continued:

> *The* Football Mail *is acknowledged to be the only representative football journal in the South of England.'*

The newspaper carried on giving a strong emphasis to football coverage through the separate *Football Mail* after the demise of RA. A wire link was set up from the paper's Edinburgh Road offices in the town centre to Fratton Park as soon as the ground was opened. But, unlike the football club, the newspaper's days were numbered. Early in 1902, the *Portsmouth Evening News* boasted that its *Football News* would include a full report of Pompey games and all other local matches, results of league matches and up to date tables. A year later, it was launched as a special edition – on green paper. *The Football News* added to the growing influence of the *Portsmouth Evening News* in the ratings war with the *Southern Daily Mail*, which the press magnate Alfred Harmsworth had established as its chief rival.

The two newspapers amalgamated on January 14, 1905, with the *Portsmouth Evening News* as the dominant partner and the one whose name has survived on a daily newspaper almost a hundred years later. But it is the *Football Mail* – not the *Football News* – whose title is a byword for Saturday night sports journalism along the south coast.

And it was in the *Football Mail* that RA's place in the footballing history of Portsmouth was acknowledged some 50 years after the team's rapid demise. The newspaper's reporter "Ranger" gave his personal opinion of The Gunners' significance to Pompey's golden jubilee celebrations in November 1948:

'The RA, due to the enthusiasm of Lt Fred Windrum and Sgt R. Bonney (subsequently Pompey's manager) suddenly sprung into prominence and fought their way through the Army Cup and other competitions and finally in 1897/98 entered and won, with 39 points out of a possible 44, the second division of the Southern League.

'This was an amateur club and when, in 1898/99, they went away for special training for a cup tie, the authorities deprived them of their amateur status and that was the end of the RA team. However, from the seed they had sown a rich harvest was to be reaped. They had created a demand and that demand had to be met. Professionalism had been making great strides all over the country. Southampton had been running a successful side for some time.

'And it was thought the time was ripe for a start to be made in Portsmouth. From the remainder of the RA team, sprung the now world-famous Pompey.'

This is RA's story.

RA were unable to live up to the good luck message of the Southern Daily Mail in 1896....

... Still going strong more than a hundred years after its first edition, the Sports Mail *has a firm place in the Saturday routine of thousands of soccer enthusiasts around Portsmouth. The newspaper was started, in September 1898, by the Southern Daily Mail to cater for the growing interest in the fortunes of RA. Its continued existence is another legacy of The Gunners a century on from the club's effective demise.*

Setting the Scene

RA's was a short life, but an illustrious one. Just seven years encompassed the history of the club. That short period was spectacular enough to lay a foundation for football in Portsmouth which has endured to the brink of the 21st Century. National cup finals, league titles and international recognition were all won, as The Gunners put Portsmouth on the football map. The current professional club, formed after RA had shown the backing that would exist in Portsmouth for a successful side, went on to become one of the biggest in the domestic game either side of the Second World War as they followed the trail blazed by RA in football's formative years in the city.

The pace at which the sport became established in the country's premier naval port was rapid. Just over 50 years covered RA's formation and Pompey's double championships. But what a tumultuous period the beginning of that era was. RA emerged from a football scene in Portsmouth where their rivals were neighbourhood sides of the likes of Southsea Rovers, Connaught Rangers and Portsmouth Wanderers. None has left any trace of its existence except, perhaps, for an inscription on an old sporting trophy. RA are the exception. Even the club's headquarters and ground still survive in the centre of Portsmouth.

The secret of that permanence a century on from their exploits stems from the side's military connections. Unlike naval outfits, army teams were free of the handicap of having to spend several months at a time at sea. And the catchment area for RA's players was, literally, the whole country rather than the narrow confines of Portsea Island.

The recruitment policy was to cause controversy when The Gunners began to dominate army football. But the club, and their founders, had by then achieved their aim. They had become one of the service's foremost sides since the Royal Engineers had monopolised the early years of the FA Cup 20 years previously.

RA's formation was probably due to a desire to create a crack military team capable of taking on the best in the south. What is definitely known concerns soccer's early beginnings in Portsmouth being fostered by the energy of a handful of stalwarts, cup rivalry and visits by some famous Scottish football-loving regiments who were occasionally quartered in the many barracks around the town.

Football made great headway among the soldiers. In 1891, a notable series of matches between the Portsmouth town club and Oxford Light Infantry created such local excitement the game's development can be accurately dated from them. The clubs contested a cup final four times before the Portsmouth side won the trophy by a single goal. But the lack of a good central ground caused the club to decline in spite of the interest in football it had helped to foster. They were survived by a crowd of junior outfits and a young football association which began to grow and flourish.

All suffered from the shortage of playing space. It was left to another military club to overcome that problem – at the United Services' Men's Ground (USMG) and the Officers' Ground (USOG) in Burnaby Road – and lead the way to a more important standing for Portsmouth in the growing world of football.

Early 1894

RA emerged after the military sides, 15th Co RA and Depot RA, had become two of the strongest teams in the Portsmouth area as the 1890s progressed. 15th Co RA, at Fort Fareham, and the Gosport-based Depot RA were given prominence in the fledgling football coverage of the *Portsmouth Evening News.*

The sports reporting in the newspaper, which was only in its second decade, was evolving as the strength of soccer's following among its readers became apparent. But its growing number of match reports of local league games and amateur players failed to disguise how far behind Portsmouth had fallen in football development compared to its great rival port of Southampton.

Even as RA were being formed, Southampton, despite having the smaller population, gained the prestige of having its own professional club when the amateurs of Southampton St Mary's decided to join the paid-up ranks ten years after their formation.

The Gunners made up for lost time by becoming the first side from either town to achieve national success. Their leadership of Sergeant Major Fred Windrum and Sergeant Richard Bonney quickly led them to a series of important honours. At least one trophy of national or local consequence was taken back every year to their base at Cambridge Barracks in Portsmouth High Street, close to their ground. Such success was a long way removed from the 15th Co RA and Depot RA's fixtures as 1894 began.

Royal Marine Artillery, RN Hospital Haslar, and Portsmouth Garrison were among the opponents. All were despatched in defeat by 15th Co RA and Depot RA. The promise of greater times to come was also shown by a 3-1 away win by 15th Co RA at Southampton St Mary's Antelope Ground on January 29. *The Portsmouth Evening News* described the clash as a 'fantastic game' with both sides fielding their strongest sides before a crowd which it said 'resembled a large concourse of people'.

Two weeks later, Depot RA of Gosport took on Southampton St Mary's at the USMG and fought out a goalless draw. The flexible nature of service football, in pre-RA days, was evident in the make-up of the Depot team. Its goalkeeper Reilly, full-backs Harms and Logan, centre-back Patterson and Maxwell and Hanna in the forward line also turned out for other variously-named service teams before they went on to play a prominent part in The Gunners' surge through the footballing ranks.

Four days on and Reilly (spelt as Riley), Harms, Logan and Patterson played in Depot RA (Rowner)'s challenge cup match at the USMG when they were on the losing side by 2–1 to 15th Co RA in a midweek fixture. A Portsmouth FA District Cup semi-final on February 17 saw a combination of those players back in action at the Men's Ground for the Depot Southern District (RA) team.

Southampton St Mary's again provided the opposition. They won 3–1 but only after the Depot had two 'goals' disallowed to the dismay of a good-sized crowd which had braved the heavy rain. Maxwell capped the Depot's performance with a goal amid great enthusiasm after St Mary's had taken a 3–0 half-time lead, though the efforts by Hanna and Scott in netting were ruled out as play became fast and furious.

The making of RA's future successes continued to become apparent as the 1893/94 season progressed. But the controversy and sportsmanship which dogged their history also came to the fore. Centre-forward Hanna, the deputy captain, had a 'little misunderstanding' with the referee according to the newspapers during a game at Cowes.

The incident led to a suspension for part of the 1894/95 season. Such events on the Isle of Wight were to be a recurring feature of The Gunners' history.

RA (Gosport) had Hanna, Maxwell and a player given as Simpson, who was probably Sampson, on the scoresheet as they reached the Army Cup semi-final with a 3–1 fifth round win at Leyton against the 1st Royal Scottish Fusiliers on February 20.

The cup draw six days later pitched the team, reported then as Depot RA, with the 2nd Battalion Gordon Highlanders at the neutral venue of Derby. Matters of a more domestic nature early the next month saw 15th Co RA's 'A' and 'B' teams reach the final of the first six-a-side tournament to be held in Portsmouth. The 'A' team were 2–1 extra-time winners after the end of the normal time of 10 minutes for each half found the sides locked on a goal apiece.

15th Co RA ended March living up to their billing as Royal Artillery Cup favourites with a 4–0 win over 4th Co Golden Hill (IoW) to retain the trophy and record their third success in its 15-year history.

Meanwhile, Depot RA (Gosport) had more prominent cups on their minds. Their 4–1 victory in the Army Cup semi-final put them in line for a final appearance against fellow Gosport side, 2nd Black Watch.

A 15,000-strong crowd gathered at Aldershot on April 4 to see the Depot team twice take the lead before they finished a remarkable game the losers by seven goals to two. Maxwell and Hanna were the Depot's scorers.

Maxwell put them in front after a move which involved Hanna. The Bombardier restored his side's lead, following a Black Watch equaliser, when he was in a good position to net from a pass from his number eight, Sampson. Going behind again spurred Black Watch into devastating action.

They moved into a 4–2 interval lead and came up against a determined Reilly in the Depot goal before a fifth goal midway through the second half and two late efforts secured the cup and brought 1893/94 to an end.

Black Watch had previously won the cup, rated more highly at the time than the later more well-known Amateur Cup, in 1889/90. But the time to emulate their success was fast approaching for many of the Depot RA's team of:

Gnr Reilly (goalkeeper), Bbr Harms, Gnr Logan (backs), Gnr Duff, Tpr Williams, Gnr Patterson (half-backs), Gnr Scott, Gnr Sampson, Bbr Hanna, Gnr Maxwell and Cpl Harrison (forwards). Some match reports had Cpl Morrison in place of Harrison.

· C H A P T E R   F I V E ·

September 1894 – April 1895

Work on RA's formation was underway as 1894/95 began and was not the friendly merger between the 15th Co RA and Depot RA which is often written about. The first mention of RA, which used the club's full name of RA (Portsmouth), appeared in the September 29 edition of the weekly *Portsmouth Times*. It commented about how one of 15th Co's early season opponents in a packed season had let the club down:

> *'The RA (P), however, agreed to fill the vacancy but on the morning of the match they also scratched and the 15th Co were left without an opponent.'*

In the following two editions, the situation about RA became clearer: *'The statement that the Depot RA will have no team this year is borne out by the fact last season's finalists have not entered for the Army Cup,'* the edition of October 6 stated. *'Several of the men have been drafted away, but one or two at least will be found playing for other teams in the district. This will be the case with RA (P) representing the gunners in Cambridge Barracks.'* The next week, with RA drawn away to Royal Marine Artillery in their first Army Cup tie, the newspaper continued:

> *'The Depot's loss was good to the Portsmouth RA. The team includes several of the Depot team who fought in the final of the Army Cup last season. On Saturday, they gained a narrow victory over the grammar school.'*

Sergeant Williams scored one of the two second-half goals in RA's first match.

The 2–0 win at the USMG, on October 6, was RA's first game. The winning start was secured with Hill and Sgt Williams the scorers after a goalless first half. The team was Riley, Phillips, Williams, Sgt Roberts, Patterson, Hill, Robertson, Howes, Sgt Williams, Samson, Pugh.

That Army Cup first round tie against RMA on October 23 was RA's initial competitive fixture. The game was again at the Men's Ground and the site – now the home of the Navy's physical training section of HMS Temeraire – was about to become the foremost sports venue in Portsmouth.

A single goal victory took The Gunners over the first hurdle. Inside-forward Samson was the scorer as the ball was laid back to him from a corner and he sent a shot past the visitors' keeper in the first half.

An 8–1 victory over United Victorias in early November gave RA their biggest win of the initial season. They were beginning

K E V I N   S M I T H   **21** to get noticed. Soon after, the Portsmouth Times penned this praise for RA and particularly their keeper:

> *'They are a very fair team indeed and have the advantage of Reilly's services in goal.'*

But they were denied an early chance to pit their emerging skills against 15th Co. A heavy downpour saw their Artillery Cup first round tie at Fareham Recreation Ground, in Bath Lane, with their established opponents abandoned after 20 minutes with the score at 0–0.

The replay ended RA's interest in the competition. They lost to three first-half goals as the 15th Co kept up their season's impressive record of P13 W11 D1 L1 F63 A6. A recollection of the matches came to light more than half a century later to reveal the bitterness between the two teams. Ex-15th Co man James Tatton, of Martin Road, Cosham, was still sore about the raw deal 15th Co were given by RA's formation. He arrived at Cambridge Barracks from Leith Fort in March 1890 and, almost 60 years on, was crystal clear about the purpose of RA's formation so soon after 15th Co's six-a-side win in 1893/94:

> *'The RA P was really formed to crush a company team, the old 15th Co SDRA, whose record from 1891 until they went to South Africa in December 1899 was outstanding. They (15th Co SDRA) won the six-a-side competition in Drill Hall against all-comers and, the following year, the six-a-side at Stamshaw and the United Services' six-a-side on the US Ground. They won the RA Cup seven years running and also won the Hants Charity Cup.*

> *When a Hampshire Senior Cup tie against RA P had to be abandoned at Fareham, owing to a gale, three of our team got in a spot of trouble and were finished with football. The old 15th Co was a siege company and while we were away at Lydd, in Kent, in the summer the RA P 'stole' another three players from us - Cook (c-f), Harper (left h-b) and McDonald (i-l). In spite of all this, 15th Co took on the RA P with all their stars in the final of the Portsmouth Cup and beat them 1–0. The old 15th Co also played in the Amateur Cup and RA P asked if Haxton (c-f) and Phinn (i-l) could play for them. It was agreed and they helped to get them to the final. As there were medals for the runners-up, Haxton was dropped in order to play a Portsmouth man and the RA were beaten 1–0.'*

Whatever ill-feeling existed between the sides, RA soon served notice of their intention to become the Portsmouth area's dominant football side, military or civilian. Just four days after their cup defeat, they were described as being 'masters of the game' and attracted a great deal of interest at the USMG to see them gain a 3–0 win over their service rivals RMA. But the early success served to prompt the first of several calls for improved off-the-pitch facilities to match the performances. The *Portsmouth Times* said:

Players 1894–1895

Allen, Bbr
Arnold
Brogue
Doyle
Fletcher, J. Gnr
Finn/Phinn, W.
Hogg, Gnr
Harms/Harmes, H.P. Bbr
Hanna/Hannah, John Bbr
Hill, William Gnr
Howes
Haig
Jardine, D. Gnr
Kinsman/Kingsman, T. Gnr
Leonard
Lavery
Maxwell, William Gnr
Moss
Moore
Newey
Patterson, William Gnr
Phillips, Davie Gnr
Phinn/Finn, W.
Pugh
Reilly/Riley, Matt Gnr
Roberts, Sgt
Robertson
Rigby
Samson/Sampson
Scott
Williams, Sgt
Williams, E.
Walsh, Paddy Cpl

RA's treasurer and trainer throughout the club's history was Regimental Sergeant Major Fred Windrum.

RA' secretary was the hard-working and energetic Sergeant Richard Bonney. He had help in the shape of Quarter Master Sergeant W.J. Manley for the 1897/98 season at least.

First team captain throughout RA's history was Sergeant John Hanna. His vice-captain was Gunner Matt Reilly, also known as 'Mick' or 'Ginger'.

Captain of the reserves was Gunner J. Fletcher. His vice-captain was Gunner Johnny McNeill, though it is unclear if they constantly occupied the positions.

'It's suggested that in view of the many important matches to be played on the Men's Ground during the season some little accommodation might be made for visitors.

At present, the spectator, after paying for admission, has to stand and watch the game on damp mud. Boards or gratings around the field of play would be greatly appreciated. Goal nets on every pitch, instead of just the principal one, would also be welcomed.'

The newspaper's plea was answered within two weeks.

Mid-December saw RA's first recorded four-figure attendance, after less than two months in existence. Some 1,500 spectators gathered at the USMG to watch the side's second round Portsmouth Senior Cup tie with the Lancaster (King's Own) Regiment. But a first-minute goal and a strong wind combined to send The Gunners tumbling out of the foremost local competition. The King's Own took full advantage of the fresh breeze behind them to quickly go ahead when left-winger Bunting sent a long shot past Reilly. RA battled against the wind to get back into the match. They kept the interval score down to that solitary goal.

But their hopes of capitalising on the weather died along with the wind. To add to their misery, Bunting went on to notch a hat-trick and Ward added another goal for the King's Own to condemn RA to a 4–0 defeat. The game took place on a special pitch laid out alongside the grandstand used for military sports days. The year ended with The Gunners in better spirits. A battling three-goal fightback in an away friendly against Bournemouth saw them turn round a two-goal half-time deficit to a 3–2 victory.

1895 began with Hanna scoring a brace of goals to help the Portsmouth FA side to a 4–3 away win over their counterparts from Brighton. The forward was among a quartet of RA players in the Pompey representative team. He was joined by Reilly, Patterson and Williams on one of the many occasions The Gunners were amply represented in either the town or county side. RA supplied the equal largest contingent in the team along with their recent opponents, the King's Own. Hanna netted another pair of goals soon after as RA decisively beat Army Service Corps 7–0. But the club were facing a problem familiar to many in the days when leagues were few and far between.

Sgt Bonney was forced to appeal for fixtures to fill vacant dates between mid-January and early February. However, RA's status in the local game was growing rapidly. It was formally recognised by their inclusion on a list of 14 clubs affiliated to the Hampshire FA. But they were not invincible.

A cross-Solent trip to take on Cowes in mid-February ended in a 2–1 defeat. It proved to be the start of a jinx which the island side exerted over the fortunes of The Gunners throughout their history.

The setback was only temporary for the Artillerymen. 15th Co RA (Fareham) were defeated 2–0 in an Army Cup fourth round tie at the Men's Ground to allow the new club to gain revenge for the cup defeat three months earlier. A crowd of some 1,500 watched Walsh and Hanna settle the game with goals either side of the interval.

The win was quickly followed by another convincing triumph in the cup. Favourites West Kent Regiment were the victims – 3–0 in the fifth round. The away game at Liverpool earned wider recognition for The Gunners. According to the *Portsmouth Times*.

'Several of the artillery team pleased the Liverpool critics not a little and more than one was invited to "sign on" Portsmouth were naturally a good deal elated with their easy victory over West Kent Regiment at Liverpool. The West Kents won the cup after a tough fight with the Sherwood Foresters in 1893 and they were not a little fancied for the trophy this year.'

RA's growing strength could also be seen with the fielding of two sides in Portsmouth's annual six-a-side tournament at North End Recreation Ground in early March. The misnamed 'B' side of Reilly, Phillips, Patterson, Williams, Jardine and Hanna won the trophy with a repeat victory over 15th Co. The winning margin on that occasion to deny the 15th Co was six points, a goal and two corners, to two points for two corners.

The 'B' team had easily reached the final with a series of emphatic victories in the early rounds. There was no such joy for the 'A' side. They fell at the first hurdle to Sandown Bay 'B'.

Three weeks later saw RA provide almost half the Hampshire side which defeated Middlesex 2–1 in a SE Counties championship clash in London. Of The Gunners' quintet, Reilly was singled out in the post-match comments for making several fine saves.

His goalkeeping skills were to be publicly applauded on many occasions to come. RA's other representatives were Harms (back), Patterson (half-back) and forwards McDonald and Hanna.

Reilly again emerged with special credit on April 3 as RA's ascendancy to the claim of being the leading side around Portsmouth gathered pace in an Army Cup semi-final versus Royal Scots Fusiliers. His several splendid saves in the first half allowed RA to change over level and pull themselves back into the game.

Hanna struck the winning goal in the 95th minute, after normal time had ended without any score, to take The Gunners into the final of the prestigious competition at the first attempt. Played at Guildford, it was never a classic game. Neither side was reported as showing much combination which, added to their generally weak shooting, created lacklustre displays.

GLORY GUNNERS

by

Kevin Smith

Football in Portsmouth owes everything to the Glory Gunners of the Royal

Artillery team -

The world-famous Pompey nickname;

The equally well-known Pompey Chimes;

The first Saturday evening sports newspaper in Portsmouth;

The first national cup wins and league titles for the city;

The first football idol;

And the first international player.

GLORY GU

by
Kevin Smith

NNERS

he History of Royal
illery (Portsmouth) FC

£6 60

Their reputation for winning brought them nationwide publicity. But a bad press was as common as a good one.

For the Artillerymen also highlighted the least savoury aspects of the game.

The club's short but colourful time at the top was ended a hundred years ago by the Football Association in a controversial row over illegal expenses for players.

The dispute was seen as a national test case between the opposing sides of the professionalism v amateurism divide.

RA's career has been hidden since their heyday to obscure the successes and scandals which went with their role as Portsmouth's best football team.

Journalist Kevin Smith has extensively researched late 19th Century archives to present the only definitive history of RA complete with comprehensive statistics.

April 1895 – Army Cup Winners

Nevertheless, 12 days later, The Gunners reached new heights in their first Army Cup final. They went from their formation to winning the national trophy with a two-goal victory in just six months. It was an unexpected success. RA were behind both the King's Own Regiment – about to reach the Amateur Cup semi-final – and the 15th Co RA in the Portsmouth soccer hierarchy, according to the *Portsmouth Times*, in every respect except goalkeeping. *'Still, pluck and dash go a long way in cup ties and the artillery have plenty of these characteristics,'* it said. But the newspaper also sounded a perceptive note of warning as the big match approached:

'The artillery are training now. But, at the same time, the men are continuing their military duty. This is as it should be. The Army Cup was instituted to encourage football amongst soldiers, not to encourage corps to keep football teams.'

Just one appearance was all it took to earn Bombardier Allen a special place in RA's history. That sole appearance came in their 1894/95 Army Cup final success against 2nd Black Watch.

The 41 words were the start of a recurrent theme throughout The Gunners' life and one which was to end it. Their cup final opponents, 2nd Black Watch, had eight of the side which had won the competition the previous season against Depot RA (Gosport). They were shocked as the Portsmouth version of The Gunners, with six of the Depot's side from a year earlier, held on to the lead provided by two second-half goals. Hanna opened the scoring with a splendid cross-shot five minutes after the interval. The cheering had barely died away before he almost increased the lead a minute later.

His performance was described as being like a tower of strength. He was joined by Harms, Phillips and Williams in turning in good displays. The Gunners' rearguard survived an onslaught by Black Watch, who were even boosted by a change in the wind direction 20 minutes from the end. But it was RA who ended the game the stronger side. Hanna capped his brilliant display when he netted for a second time ten minutes from the end. Lady Butler, the wife of 2nd Infantry Brigade commander General Sir William Butler, presented the cup and medals to the winners to complete an afternoon of excitement for the 12,000 crowd. It had begun with hundreds of fans travelling from Portsmouth to Aldershot at noon. RA arrived in the early afternoon and were driven in a dray to the ground from the Flying Horse pub.

Their opponents had stayed with the Argyll and Sutherland Highlanders in Aldershot for two days. They appeared first on the pitch, being led on by a piper from the Argyll and Sutherland to loud cheers. RA followed soon after and began by kicking into the strong easterly wind. Early play was lively and both keepers were in action. The Black Watch then 'netted' only for the effort to be disallowed for an illegal charge on Reilly.

Black Watch continued to have most of the opening play. Reilly had to save well from a shot by Geary. But The Gunners' opener seemed to put them well on top and apparently bound for an easy victory. Their opponents hit back only to be foiled by a combination of Reilly's skills and bad finishing. Hanna's second goal sealed the Portsmouth side's victory.

RA's feat was recorded at great length by *The Times* but the newspaper said the victory owed less to their skills than the shortcomings of their opponents. 'It is questionable whether the better side won,' noted its reporter:

> 'The wind was strong and spoilt the short passing game of the losers, whose forwards got into a very good game in the first half. But The Gunners took the full benefit of a brilliant and skilful defence. Reilly more than demonstrated his force as a goalkeeper and the result could pretty well be brought home to his play in goal. Repeatedly, Black Watch seemed on the point of equalizing but Reilly and a lack of good fortune with Black Watch created a feeling the game was not for them.'

For RA, he said:

> 'Philips and Harms were very sure at full-back and, in the first half, did work well in thwarting the Black Watch attack. The wind blew from goal to goal and, as a team with this advantage, Black Watch ought to have played better. However, RA deserve every credit for keeping their goal intact and, with the wind behind them, quickly generated a wonderful game.'

The theme was continued by the *Portsmouth Times*:

> 'Black Watch spared no training to ensure a second success in the Army Cup. The Artillery are without a doubt a winning team in cup ties. Since Christmas they have knocked out the 15th Co, West Kent Rgt, Scots Fusiliers and 2nd Black Watch, certainly four of the strongest combinations in the army.'

RA had Reilly to thank for the cup, while Hanna, the half-backs and Harms – whose form varied from feebleness to brilliancy – also earned praise from the newspaper.

The Times noted the final as RA's second in succession. While strictly untrue, this acknowledged the fact the cup final side was similar to the RA (Gosport) team which had faced Black Watch the previous year. Reilly, Harms, Patterson, Williams, Hanna, and Maxwell played both games for the RA side. Hanna scored on both occasions.

The full 1895 final line-up was: Gnr Reilly, Gnr Phillips, Bbr Harms, Gnr Patterson, Gnr Hogg, Gnr Kinman, Gnr Jardine, Bbr Hanna, Sgt Williams, Bbr Allen, Gnr Maxwell.

Black Watch: L-Cpl Gill, L-Sgt Fairweather, Pt Barr, L-Sgt Bissett, Pt Crawford, Pt Clarke, Pt Geary, Cpl Webb, Pt Docherty, Pt Connor, Pt Campbell.

RA had emerged from a large entry of 64 teams to become the seventh winners of the Army Cup. It was a magnificent trophy. An Army sports publication from the 1930s gave this fulsome description:

> 'The AFA Challenge trophy is a silver replica of the famous Warwick vase, made in the year 1838, being the work of one Paul Storr, a famous silversmith of that time. The vase was purchased in 1888. This grand antique Bacchanalian vase is now in possession of the Earl of Warwick and stands at Warwick Castle in a conservatory specially built to contain it. The vase is of white

marble and of massive proportions, measuring 5ft 7in in height and about 8ft across from handle to handle. The body is draped in a lion's skin and is enriched on the one side with four satyrs' heads and on the reverse with the heads of three satyrs and one bacchante. It stands on a square foot, whilst underneath the body and springing from the foot is a beautiful piece of acanthus leafwork. The handles are formed of twisted vine branches, which are carried round the mouth and at various intervals are suspended clusters of grapes and vine leaves. The vase is of Roman origin and evidently of the early part of the Second Century, being probably made during the reign of the Emperor Hadrian (AD 117–138), who is noted as a great patron of the arts and literature. It was discovered in 1770 in the precincts of the villa of Hadrian, near Tivoli, that celebrated storehouse of treasures of art.

A satyr is a Greek god of the woodlands, while a bacchante is a priestess of Bacchus, the god of wine. The vase passed into the Warwick family by marriage. The authorative *Book of Football*, published in 1906, was of a similarly appreciative mood, though its description differed slightly:

'It is of solid silver and very massive. The workmanship is a fine specimen of the silversmith's art, being skilfully executed in every detail. The cup stands on a square silver pedestal and the height is 20ins.'

RA's achievement in the cup had created a record. *The Portsmouth Evening News* reported that their success was based on a solid defence and the solitary goal they conceded in six games in becoming cup-holders was unsurpassed. But The Gunners seemed to have an even better record than that. None of their opponents – 15th Co RA, King's Royal Rifles, Royal Marine Artillery, West Kent Regiment, Scots Fusiliers and Black Watch – appeared to have scored against them. The confusion could have arisen because RA received a bye in the second round, while the 15th Co RA were beating the Royal Lancaster Regiment 3–1.

Though RA were the best side around Portsmouth, the 15th Co RA could also celebrate local successes. They won the RA Challenge Cup for the fourth year in a row and the Hampshire Charity Cup. The season ended with the cup wins and the summer, as with all those in the mid–1890s, was devoid of footballing news.

A first trophy in their first season saw PA pose proudly for their first known team photograph.

September – December 1895

The opening of the 1895/96 season saw one of the most severe reversals of fortunes possible for RA. They suffered a 6–1 rout away to Luton Town on September 14. Only the performance of left-winger Meggs, with his frequent brilliant runs, allied to RA's inventive style, could give any early comfort to the side's fans for the season ahead. A 0–0 draw away to London Welsh followed, with Reilly lavishly praised, before an appeal was issued for The Gunners to have a private ground where they could play the leading sides at home.

Mindful, perhaps, of how a suitable venue was the downfall of the Portsmouth town club at the start of the decade the *Portsmouth Evening News*' reporter said the Artillerymen deserved the support of a person enterprising enough to provide them with a home to match their ambitions. Teams such as Luton Town and New Brompton, now Gillingham, had to be taken on away, he wrote.

> *'With such a team as RA in Portsmouth, we could get some splendid games here if only we had a private ground where the club could get a gate.'*

The situation led RA to wherever they would be offered a 'sensible sum' guaranteed for their expenses. They could not do otherwise, he added. They could not afford to pay their costs to away games and they did not get a profit from their fixtures in Portsmouth.

RA's next journey, to Freemantle, brought them a 4–1 win as September drew to a close. RA topped that win with ten-man victories against RMA (2–0) and Dublin Fusiliers (6–0), Cook and MacDonald going off injured in the games to cut short their returns to the side. Against the Fusiliers, however, RA were as convincing as the scoreline suggested. They out-fought and out-played the visitors for the first of two decisive victories against them in a fortnight. Reading, who had recently turned professional, were too strong for RA soon afterwards, however. But, once more, the 3–0 defeat took place away, with The Gunners' lack of a home ground evident.

The Artillerymen made light of the difficulty when they had the best of the game against another professional team, Tottenham Hotspur, to win 2–1. A Maxwell goal after eight minutes and Cook, netting five minutes from time, sealed the away victory on October 27. RA were in good heart to begin the defence of the Army Cup with a 5–0 win. Dublin Fusiliers were again the victims before The Gunners notched up a record 10–0 win at home to Clifton in the Amateur Cup qualifying competition's second round on November 2.

Left-half, Gunner William Patterson – one of RA's most loyal players.

The Gunners had received a bye in the first round and the next hurdle proved almost as easy to overcome. The game was all over by the interval which RA reached seven goals in front. It was so one-sided, it was uninteresting for the 2,000 spectators. But what a way to start the month.

RA's place in Portsmouth's soccer establishment was confirmed a few days later. Sgt Bonney, the club's secretary, was chosen for the Portsmouth Football Association's executive. Within a week, it was Reilly who was again attracting the headlines. The flamboyant keeper took his tactic of running a considerable distance with the ball and dropping it on the ground into his side's fixture at Bristol South End, the forerunners of Bristol City. The custodian's method was well-known around Portsmouth but had never before been seen in the West Country. It caused considerable interest but could not help his side to a win. The match ended in a goalless draw. Controversy of a more serious nature loomed, however, as was so often the case in RA's existence.

Truth magazine, a Victorian sporting publication, used a mid-November edition just after the first anniversary of RA's formation to complain about what it alleged was a manufactured team. Its indignant writer moaned:

'The 15th Co RA have a very successful football team which was formed at considerable expense and, last year, it covered itself with glory. Two of its crack players have been transferred to other companies in Portsmouth with the object, so we are led to believe, of securing their services for a new team called Royal Artillery, Portsmouth, which is supposed to be in the running for the Army Cup. The 15th, who were in round five of the Army Cup last year, and were expected to do better still this season, were consequently highly indignant.

'It seems a queer state of things that transfers should be manipulated solely with an eye to results on the football field. But there really appears to be some reason for supposing that this is done. I hear, in one case, a crack football player was transferred from the south of England to the north which, naturally, he did not like. But he got a hand from Portsmouth. If he chose to apply to that quarter, there would be a transfer. Sure enough, within a few weeks, he found his way to Portsmouth and was playing for a team there. It is nothing short of a scandal that the public purse should be put to the expense of shunting men about in this way. And it's also calculated to take all the esprit de corps *out of the different football teams for a club which has influence in all the right quarters to have the power of robbing all sides of their crack players.'*

Nothing official came of the protest but two cup ties between RA and two 15th Co teams within three weeks of the article were littered with bad feelings. As the match report of the first of those games – an Army Cup tie – against 15th Co RA (Gosport) commented:

'Some of the players showed a tendency to roughness and fouls were not infrequent. Referee J.P. Purnell, of Ryde, found it necessary to caution one or two of the players.'

RA survived the clashes to win 3–1 with goals from Hanna and Maggs, or Meggs, 2. The pattern was repeated the next week when RA faced the Fareham section of the 15th Co in the Hampshire Senior Cup's second round on November 30. RA centre-back Patterson was ordered off by the referee, Mr A.H. Wood, in the closing minutes for kicking an opponent.

He had earlier netted one of his side's five goals as the 15th Co crumbled in extra time. The score after 90 minutes had been a goal apiece. Two of RA's strikes came from penalties converted by Meggs – or Maggs as he was called in the match report – to also show the game's ill-tempered nature.

The hostile atmosphere spread to the crowd. A section of the spectators subjected Mr Wood to heavy barracking. In between the fixtures, RA's easy time continued in the Amateur Cup. Bristol St George's called off their intended tie on November 16 in the third round of the qualifying competition.

The next round took place at a time of a very crowded fixture list for The Gunners a year after they had been forced to tout for games. Their progress in so many contests saw them continually approach the the Portsmouth FA for permission to rearrange games. As the footballing flagship in the town, they rarely encountered any problems. RA's busy times were compounded by the fielding of a reserve side, which generally held its own against lesser clubs' first XIs in the Hampshire Junior Cup and similar competitions.

RA's successes in 1895 were attracting more attention further afield. This time, the emphasis was complimentary. *The Hampshire Telegraph* used its first edition of December to report forward and captain Hanna was wanted by West Bromwich Albion, no less. The Baggies, Football League founders, had won the FA Cup twice and were about to reach the final for a third time.

But Hanna stayed loyal to The Gunners instead of joining one of the foremost pioneering sides of organized football in England. Reilly was also the subject of interest from Midlands clubs. Derby County and Notts County, during their best league spell, wanted the keeper 'noted for his wonderful dexterity with his hands', as the *Hampshire Telegraph* described his play.

Once again, however, RA's meteoric rise had its critics. A December issue of *Athletic News* took up *Truth*'s grievance of the previous month. The latest criticism warned the Army's football chiefs their sport was heading for trouble if they were not circumspect and alert. And RA were the cause. Its report said:

> '*Difficulties first presented themselves because some enthusiasts secured the transfer from one regiment to another of a couple of men who were wanted for one of the cup teams. Of course, the teams who were poached on grumbled and got their friends to complain. Also, with regard to an attempt recently made by a Football League club to secure an Army man, this was very good to the cause of those who are seeking to make it their business to oppose all kinds of sport. It is said any repeat of the Army to put football before the usual rules will lend to an appeal to the "authorities".*'

The theme of army footballers being classed as amateurs, a recurring thread throughout RA's history, was willingly taken up again by *Truth* magazine the following week.

It used The Gunners' emphatic 5–1 home triumph over Old Weymouthians in the Amateur Cup's final qualifying round in between the latest articles to justify its further attack. Some 2,000 spectators celebrated as two goals from Hanna and one apiece from Jardine, Patterson and Kinman brought RA a tie against the 3rd

Players 1895–1896

Brazier, Gnr
Cook/Cooke Gnr
Doyle
Fletcher, J. Gnr
Hanna/Hannah, John Bbr
Harms/Arms, H.R. Bbr
Harper Gnr
Haxton, Micky Gnr
Hill, William Gnr
Hooper
Hogg/Hoff Gnr
Harness
Harrison, E.
Jackson
Jardine, D. Gnr
Kinman, T. Gnr
Little
Maxwell, William Gnr
Meggs/Maggs, James Gnr/Bbr
McNeill/McNeil, Johnny Gnr
McDonald Gnr
Patterson/Batterson, William Gnr
Reilly/Ryley, Matt Gnr
Stewart Gnr
Tyre, G.J.
Williams Sgt
Welsh/Walsh, Paddy Cpl
Walton

Grenadiers in the first round proper in their debut season in a nationwide competition. But *Truth* saw little to be happy about:

> *'It's bound to become a serious question before long,' the magazine wrote, 'as to whether Army teams can play for the Amateur Association Cup. Both RA and Royal Scots won their ties. The majority of Army teams belong to a class of men, respectable enough in other ways, who supply the professional teams.*

> *'Apart from that, their occupations tend to physical development and they have opportunities for training provided for them in a way which gives them an enormous advantage over ordinary amateurs for whom the cup was intended. Then, too, there would be quite enough football among Army teams without going any further afield. The fact such teams enter for this cup is another illustration of the inevitable way the game is being overtaken by the Army.'*

On the football pitch meanwhile, RA shrugged aside the controversy to end 1895 as it began. Six of the club's players (keeper Reilly, back Phillips, half-backs Patterson and Harper, right-winger Meggs and forward Hanna) dominated the line-up of the Portsmouth FA's team for the new year's fixture against their Brighton counterparts.

The Gunners' contingent played a decisive part in the Pompey side's 5–0 victory. Meggs scored two goals, with another coming from Hanna courtesy of a Patterson centre, while Reilly kept a clean sheet.

· C H A P T E R   E I G H T ·

January – March 1896

Whatever RA's players and officials thought of the criticisms against them, they did not allow themselves to be distracted from the business of scoring goals and winning games in the early days of 1896. They beat Southsea Rovers 6–0 in the Portsmouth Senior Cup's second round to leave the local paper happy with the first half of the season:

'RA have no cause to be dissatisfied with their record. They have never had a proper team on the field this season and now have three men, Cook, MacDonald and Harper, hors de combat. 'Notwithstanding this, they have done well: P15 W9 Dl L5 F46 A24,'

commented the *Portsmouth Evening News*. The paper reported that RA's reserves had enjoyed even greater success. They had maintained a 100 per cent record from their 13 games, with 46 goals scored and only 9 conceded. Their season had begun with a 4–1 win over RA Hilsea and continued with wins of 6, 7, 8–0 in some cases.

But the middle of January onwards saw RA's fortunes suffer a setback. They could only manage a goalless draw with Weymouth Athletic. A walk-over had been expected. Lacklustre wins were recorded over Cowes and Portsmouth Wanderers before RA were held to a 1–1 draw by the 3rd Grenadier Guards in the Amateur Cup.

Upwards of 4,000 people created RA's biggest crowd to date as Meggs gave the home team a good start with a 10th-minute goal. His side failed to build on the lead, however, and Molyneaux put the Guards level before half-time. The fast and furious play continued after the break, though the second period was as noticeable for a further confirmation of Reilly's reputation as anything else. His flamboyance on one occasion saw him run a great distance, handling the ball, before he put it away to safety with a hefty kick. The 90 minutes ended with a draw and a replay was needed after the Guards refused to play extra time.

The Morning Leader considered the game a more stirring battle than Leander Jameson's raid from Mafeking to Transvaal in southern Africa to overthrow the government and support the area's non-Boer colonists. RA had more mundane matters on their minds instead of such hyped-up praise. They protested to the cup's emergency committee in an attempt to get the replay with the Guards scratched in their favour. The Gunners' grievance centred on the fact they were willing to play on in the original game.

But, even though the Guards' representative admitted he knew extra time had been required, the committee rejected RA's appeal. Before the replay – again at home – could take place in early February, RA's growing band of fans were reassured renewed rumours about the departures of Hanna and Reilly to the professional ranks were false.

It was Hanna who scored the second of RA's two goals in the replay with the Guards but his side were again held to a draw. The score stayed at 2–2, even though extra time was played on that occasion, before a crowd of about 5,000. But the teams were fast running out of time to decide the fixture.

Back they went to the cup committee. A three-day extension was granted. RA made the best use of it. Cook netted the only goal of the second replay, staged at Guildford, from Hanna's 25th-minute pass. The game was said to have been one of the best staged at the Surrey town. The poor attendance of 300 was put down to the fact some fans had mixed up the date and travelled to the fixture on the previous day.

The supporters were obviously lasting the pace of five gruelling and crucial games within a fortnight worse than the players who had to appear on the heavy mid-winter pitches.

In the Victorian era, as now, one of the prices of footballing success was a build-up of important fixtures, though players of a hundred years ago such as The Gunners were lacking the benefits of modern training and sports science to help them cope with the rigours of physical matches played with weighty water-absorbent leather balls and boots far removed from their modern lightweight equivalents.

RA's reward for their endeavours was known within 24 hours. It entailed a lengthy journey to the north-east to take on Amateur Cup holders Middlesborough, a side understandably described as formidable opponents. They had knocked out Portsmouth's King's Own Lancaster Regiment in the cup's semi-finals a year earlier.

The Teesside club were lying third in the Northern League. Their playing record was: P12 W6 D3 L3 F22 A16 Pts 15. But the *North-Eastern Daily Gazette* informed its readers Boro would have to beat Reilly, a keeper whose fame was spreading, if they were to defeat RA:

> *'The Artillerymen will have one of the finest custodians in the south and the team as a whole is a most exciting one. The game is exciting very considerable interest and will, no doubt, be fought with great determination by both sides.'*

The Morning Leader newspaper added to Reilly's stature in being the champion stopper of the army as it warned fans of the Black Swans, as it tagged Boro, their team faced a tough game:

> *'The holders of the cup – or rather the winners of the final tie last year – may rest assured that the soldiers will give them an excellent game. And it may be as well to remind the northerners that Reilly keeps watch for them under the bar.'*

He was only beaten once, in the second-half, as RA notched up a goal each side of half-time for a 2–1 win in their furthest away match to date. It was their fifth cup tie in February as they continued the season's triumphal march. But this progress, added to a goalless draw in the Army Cup with Royal Irish Rifles, put The Gunners' season in danger of exploding with games. They had played 26 matches to the middle of February compared to 23 during all of the previous season. Reilly's good form was one reason for the continued interest in a staggering four cups. His skills were again amply recognised in a quest by the *Morning Leader* to find the best four footballers in the South. RA's custodian was the runner-up in the poll. One of his enthusiasts wrote:

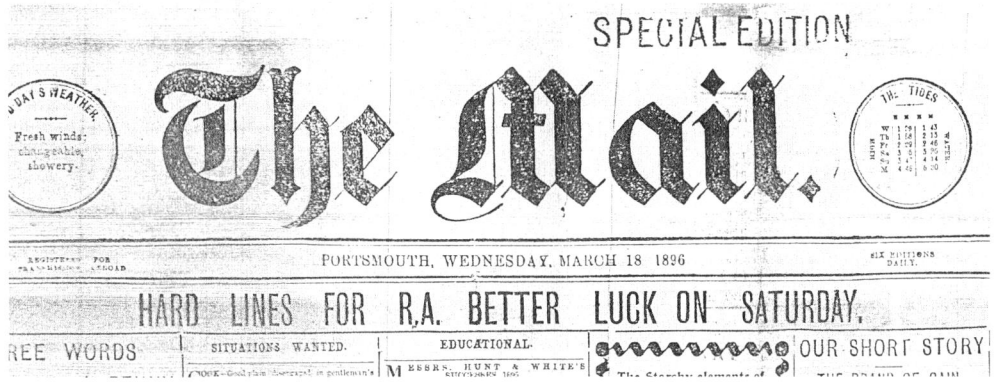

Front page news was created by RA when they relinquished their hold on the Army Cup in 1895/96.

'Good goalkeepers are common enough among soldiers and I could name six custodians at Aldershot good enough for almost any club. But after witnessing Mick's wonderful display in the final of the Army Cup for two years in a row, and dozens of other matches, I maintain the best goalkeeper in the south is found in the person of the genial young Irishman, Gnr Michael Reilly.'

Reilly was in esteemed company. He was beaten to the top spot by four times England international G.B. Raikes, of Old Carthusians, who were about to record an unprecedented double to confirm their place as one of England's top sides.

The old boys of Charterhouse public school, in Surrey, went on to claim the Amateur Cup in 1897, three years after they had first won the trophy, to add to their FA Cup triumph of 13 years earlier. Second Division Woolwich Arsenal's Fairclough occupied third place in the survey.

A crowd of more than 3,000 gathered at the US Men's Ground on February 19 to see Reilly help RA make their cluttered season even busier. They ended Royal Irish Rifles' interest in the Army Cup with a 3–1 third round replay win. The attendance was used by the Hampshire Telegraph to defend Portsmouth's football fans against a charge of apathy. The newspaper noted that RA's following compared well to average attendances in the English Cup's first and second rounds of 9,518 and 13,812:

'It is often said Portsmouth people do not appreciate sport to any degree but they are altogether very lukewarm in that matter. Portsmouth people like others, however, will turn out whenever anything good is to be seen as was instanced at the two meetings of RA and the Grenadier Guards at the Officers' Ground with respective attendances of 4,000 and 5,000. In the last week, when RA played Royal Irish Rifles in the Army Cup, there was getting on for something like 3,000 present.'

Among them was a female fan discovered by the *Portsmouth Times* on the trams as its reporter "Hotspur" commented:

'She proudly explained that she had been to every game on the Men's Ground. The passengers were treated to an eloquent discourse of the powers of the RA team, their chances for the Army Cup and the individual excellencies of the players.'

RA added to the season's successes when they overcame Freemantle 1–0 in a Hampshire Senior Cup semi-final with a 20th minute neat oblique shot by Walsh just four days after their most recent win in the Army Cup.

Several of The Gunners' first-team regulars had also been on duty in Hampshire's intervening midweek game against Dorset. The Gunners kept on course for the Portsmouth Senior Cup as well, with a 1–1 draw with Royal Marines Light Infantry. The cup games allowed the soldiers to boast an impressive record at the end of February, with 17 out of 29 games won, seven drawn and five lost. Their goals total of 73 was more than double the number conceded to give them an average scoring record of two and a half goals a game.

Maidenhead were out to ruin that record with special training sessions before the teams clashed in the Amateur Cup's third round proper. The extra work proved useless as RA – with an average height of 5ft 10in and weighing 13 stone – lived up to the pre-match prediction in the *Maidenhead Advertiser* of giving a good account of themselves with a resounding five-goal away triumph. *'RA are a sturdy lot and Maidenhead will have to go all the way to put in a game,'* the newspaper commented. An even first-half gave way to a rout for RA after the interval. The floodgates opened ten minutes after the re-start. Home full-back Lowman was in Johnson's view in goal to allow a soft shot to beat the keeper. Johnson was given little chance three minutes later when Meggs netted a penalty, awarded after he had been fouled by Gilroy. Cook added two more goals and

Hanna quickly rounded off the scoring. *The Maidenhead Advertiser* rued the fact that the home side couldn't compete with the victors:

'The best team won, of that there is no doubt. Maidenhead were completely outclassed by a team that is as good as many professional combinations.'

No match report was seemingly complete without a special mention of Reilly and that of the cup win was no exception:

'Reilly has a style of defence peculiarly his own. The rule will not allow a goalkeeper to carry the ball more than a couple of steps. So Reilly bounces it as far as it is safe for him to do so and then he punches it well away.'

The Gunners' convincing win brought them a semi-final place against Shrewsbury.

Wins in national competitions don't come much better – or bigger – than RA's ten goal drubbing of Clifton. The second round qualifying competition tie in 1895 produced the largest triumph the Artillerymen recorded in any national event.

Their opponents, previous winners of the Welsh Cup, were seen as more preferable opposition than the other semi-finalists of Bishop Auckland and Darlington. Being drawn against either of those northern outfits would have meant a longer journey for RA to the neutral venue required.

However, The Gunners' national progress was causing friction in the local footballing scene as fixtures piled up. Their Army Cup fifth-round tie away to 1st Battalion South Lancashires at Bristol caused them to appeal to the Portsmouth FA for the Portsmouth Senior Cup semi-final with the RMLI to be postponed. The Marines were unhappy with the prospect. Their representatives told the association their footballers were being moved away and RA had a clear duty to give up their rights in the Army Cup. Tempers were not eased by the PFA's decision for a further deferral of the fixture for another couple of weeks. RMLI protested strongly and threatened to withdraw from the cup. *The Portsmouth Evening News* was in no doubt the Army Cup committee was to blame for the situation. They arranged their games without any talks with the local associations. The PFA accused the committee of arrogance, especially after RA's secretary, Sgt Bonney, who was elected a vice-president of the PFA a week earlier, had told the association no deviation from the Army Cup date was allowed.

He promised RA would pay all RMLI's expenses involved in the postponement of the Portsmouth Senior Cup tie. When the Army Cup fifth round was staged, on March 4, RA put the off-field row behind them as they sought to reach the final for the second year running. They beat the 1st Battalion South Lancashires 5–2 after extra time. The teams had been level at 2–2 on 90 minutes.

A day of rain had left the ground slippery but Walsh got RA off to the perfect start with a goal within the first three minutes. He restored the lead by half-time after right-winger Fox had put the South Lancs level.

Another equaliser followed soon into the second half.

There was no further score until RA began to dominate extra time. Jardine put them in front for the third time in the game and two more goals from scrambles in front of the South Lancs' goal sealed the victory.

The Mail (Portsmouth) said the March 3 win, like that against Maidenhead, was achieved through RA possessing greater staying power than their opponents.

March–April 1896
Amateur Cup Finalists

With one final a step closer, RA found themselves in another just three days later. They defeated St Mary's Reserves 3–0 to win the 1895/96 Hampshire Senior Cup. RA were the first Portsmouth side to achieve the feat. St Mary's and Aldershot Engineers had won the cup three times each, while Freemantle and the defunct Woolston Works team each had one success to their names. The only Portsmouth-based side before The Gunners to lift any county trophy was St Simon's in 1894 in the junior version of the Hampshire Cup.

Hanna, the RA captain, received special mention for his contribution to the cup final win. *The Mail* (Portsmouth) commented:

> *'Hanna, who was rather lame, kept his men together in great style. It would be difficult to overestimate his value to the side, for in addition to his ability as a player he is a consummate general.'*

The victorious team was met at the Town Station by the band and men from Cambridge Barracks. The band struck up "See the Conquering Hero Comes" in what was to become a frequent routine. The *Brighton Evening Argus'* report of the scenes read:

> *'Nearly 300 comrades accompanied the team and they were augmented at the station by a big contingent from Cambridge Barracks and a crowd of civilians. The victors were accorded a most enthusiastic welcome. Several members of the team were carried shoulder high from the station to the barracks, where they were heartily congratulated on their victory by Colonel Wynne and the officers, who also honoured the victory in the usual way by filling the cup with champagne. Afterwards, it was taken across to the sergeants' mess and filled again. The RA have this season played 17 cup games without defeat and scored 58 goals to 12 against.'*

The next month would tell if they were going to build on that fine record and achieve a staggering three further cup triumphs during April. They heard news of their Army Cup semi-final opponents, Royal Scots at Tufnell Park in North London, as they crushed RMLI 5–0 in their controversial Portsmouth Senior Cup semi-final. About a thousand fans turned out to see the 1–1 draw in the original tie three weeks earlier decisively overturned.

Meggs put them one up in the opening minutes. It took RMLI 20 minutes to mount an attack. They shot wide and it was all RA from then on. Welsh scored their second from a scramble in front of the Marines' posts.

He added a fourth just before half-time following an effort by Cook. A neat one-two brought RA's final, and only, goal in the second half. A good pass from Phillips's free-kick saw Harms put in a good run before he released the ball for Phillips to score. RMLI had no answer.

RA's opponents in the final, as they sought to keep alive their extraordinary season, were 15th Co RA. Another game with no love lost between the rivals was in prospect. *The Hampshire Telegraph* billed the final as 'the game of the year'. It was eagerly awaited and seen as a match which would test the strength of both sides as well as proving lucrative to the Portsmouth FA's coffers: *'The big match will most likely be the only local one on that day and, given the weather, there should be a large and satisfactory "gate",'* the paper commented. Naturally enough, the final clashed with another of RA's numerous cup-ties as their campaign reached a climax. But the potentially contentious situation was defused by 15th Co. Its representative, Sgt Morgan, began to heal the rift between the two clubs when he readily agreed to a switch and refused RA's offer of compensation.

Next on RA's hectic schedule was their Army Cup semi-final on March 17. It was their 19th cup-tie of the season. They had scored 58 goals to 12 conceded in all cup competitions but their unbeaten run was to end as they sought to become the second team to retain the Army Cup.

The Royal Scots (Chatham) denied them that achievement by winning 2–1. A fast game saw the Scots two goals up at half-time, though RA had gone close when a neat shot hit the bar. The Gunners didn't go down without a fight. Hanna netted to finish off a good move between himself, Cook and Jardine. Another of his efforts was disallowed because of handball and Bignall, in the Scots' goal, kept his opponents at bay.

Centre-half Gunner Hogg was ever-present in the middle of the RA defence as the side made its way to the final of the Amateur Cup in 1895/96.

The Kent side also had their full-backs and half-backs to thank for earning them their final place after a game where defences were on top. The blame for the defeat in wet conditions was put firmly by *The Mail* (Portsmouth) on RA's crowded season:

'RA have tried for too much. Two cup-ties a week for about two months would make any team struggle. The unfortunate part of it is that, of all the trophies they were in, The Gunners would have preferred to win the Army Cup. It is to the services the highest honour and, having got it last year, they were particularly keen to keep it at Cambridge Barracks. Hanna, above all the forwards, showed his true form. Harms and Phillips showed up well and Reilly did fairly in goal. But the general impression the team gave was that they were very weak.'

The defeat brought a check to RA's triumphal season. It followed a 16-game unbeaten run and was their first loss of 1896. Their last had been against Southampton on December 28. It was not the best way for RA to approach another semi-final, this time in the Amateur Cup, four days later.

Shrewsbury, their next opposition, could also boast a more impressive record in reaching the last four of the competition. The Shrews had beaten Casuals 4–2 away, before routing Old Brightonians 6–2 at home to set up a 2–1 victory at Marlow.

By contrast, RA had taken three attempts to get past 3rd Grenadier Guards before they had gone on to two away wins, at holders Middlesborough (2–1) and Maidenhead (5–0). But The Gunners' good form on the road continued with a 2–0 victory against Shrewsbury, at the neutral venue of Reading, to reach the Amateur Cup final in only their second season.

They prepared for the semi-final with a stay at Margate. Some 1,500 spectators were present for the match at the Caversham Road ground, about to be replaced as Reading's home. Those who paid the 6d admission, with a further 6d for the enclosure, saw Walsh give RA the lead in the tenth minute.

His fine shot was missed by the Shrews' captain and back W.H. Ellis to go into the net. Cook notched the second goal after several fast exchanges. His low shot followed a nice centre from Meggs. The effort spurred Shrewsbury into action. One of their forwards, Salt, sent in a fine shot but The Gunners' defence held firm as half-time approached. Salt had bad luck in failing to score after the restart and his team continued to press as Reilly saved a splendid straight shot from centre-forward Benbow. RA held on to their lead in spite of the Shrewsbury pressure and finished 2–0 winners to secure a place in the final the following week.

Bishop Auckland were the opponents. *The Portsmouth Evening News* was confident RA would continue their footballing rise:

'...Bishop Auckland will be a thorough fight but RA have played so well throughout the season we hope, with good grounds, they will walk off with the cup.'

The Portsmouth Evening News was similarly hopeful:

'RA stand a good chance of bringing the cup to Portsmouth if they play up to their usual fashion, though their opponents will undoubtedly give them a good game.'

It went on to inform its readers that Bishop Auckland were considered to be the premier club of their district and had previously been Amateur Cup semi-finalists as well as producing consistent performances in the Durham Cup. Several ex-Bishops had also gained prominence with other clubs. Most notable among them were Welford and Chatt, who had gone on to achieve fame with Football League giants Aston Villa. Their former team-mates proved worthy of living up to their example as ten-man Bishop Auckland clinched the cup for the first time on a pitch made heavy by morning rain.

Disappointment in Portsmouth was recorded by the Hampshire Telegraph at RA's defeat in the 1895/96 Amateur Cup final by a ten-man Bishop Auckland.

The winning goal was struck before the players had settled down and took Reilly by surprise. A strong wind spoiled the game, played at Leicester Fosse on March 28, but it was considered extraordinary that RA could not defeat a side one man short for most of the match.

Foster met with a bad accident soon after Lodge had given the Bishops a fifth-minute lead from a pass by Lewin and had to retire with a broken collarbone. *The Portsmouth Evening News* continued:

'For a long time, the soldiers, who had the best advantage of a strong wind, had the best of the play. Walsh scored an offside goal, while Hanna struck the upright with a good shot. Nothing further was scored, and Bishop Auckland crossed over with the lead. Nothing was scored on either side in the second-half.'

The Portsmouth Times reported RA tried hard after the interval:

'Hanna, Cook, Jardine and Hill being conspicuous and they were certainly unlucky in not scoring. Reilly, in goal, made some winning saves.'

RA's failure to beat ten men meant the cup went to a northern England club for the second time. For the Bishops, already one of the country's leading amateur sides, a further nine successes in the cup were to follow. But they had to withstand a post-match protest from RA before they could confidently claim their initial win.

RA's close links with controversy surfaced again as they complained to the FA Council about their defeat. Sgt Fairbairn claimed the referee, R. Bourke, had cut short the first half by five minutes when RA were pressing strongly for an equalizer with the wind behind them.

A press statement seemed to back up the allegation but Mr Bourke denied being the source and said he was sure the full 45 minutes had been played. His admission that the FA's secretary, F.J. Wall, had used half-time to point out a mistake had been made and that the spectators had become angry at some issue at the match brought The Gunners no joy. The FA Council fully backed Mr Bourke.

RA's season was about to get worse. The Portsmouth Senior Cup final a fortnight later, which offered them a chance to get over their recent disappointments, ended in 15th Co RA inflicting a single-goal defeat. RA went into the game comforted by the fact they had decisively won the season's two previous cup clashes against 15th Co sides. And the teams had similar records in reaching the final:

RA – 1R – Portsmouth Town scratched;
2R – Southsea Rovers 6–0;
3R – RMLI 1–1; replay 5–0.

15th Co – 1R – Dublin Fusiliers 6–0;
2R – RMA 4–0 abandoned, darkness; replay 1–0;
s-f – Gosport Red Star 2–1.

The Gunners began the final, delayed by ten minutes because referee Mr A.H. Wood failed to turn up, by pinning their opponents in their own half only to go behind to a deflected free kick from Moorhouse which hit Phinn, the centre, to totally deceive Reilly two minutes before half-time. Only Reilly stopped 15th Co inflicting a heavy defeat on his team. The rest of The Gunners let their heads drop to end the match demoralised. It was a well-deserved win for 15th Co, according to the *Portsmouth Evening News*:

'15th Co undoubtedly secured the trophy on their merits. They displayed much of the excellent form for which they were famous when stationed at Fort Fareham two years ago, while RA were starkly deficient in combination. Sgt Morgan and his team are to be congratulated on their victory which is, of course, no light one being secured as it was by a single company against the pick of all the Southern District RA.'

The Portsmouth Times gave its description of the after-match scenes:

'The cup and medals were presented to the winners by the ex-mayor, Alderman J. King, each of the winners being heartily cheered, as was Reilly.'

The final effectively ended a season which, at one stage, saw RA poised to complete a unique set of cup wins only to end on a low note with two final defeats and a semi-final loss in a four-game spell to leave their Hampshire Senior Cup win in isolation. Their season was summed up by the *Hampshire Telegraph* as containing some 'fine times'.

A benefit match away to Southampton St Mary's closed 1895/96 with a draw of a goal apiece. A thousand or so strong crowd helped to boost the funds for the spectators injured by the collapse of a roof at the English Cup tie between Saints and Sheffield Wednesday earlier in the season.

Pre-season – November 1896 Table-Toppers

R A's spirits were heartened for the coming season by an FA decision for once in their favour. They were granted an exemption from the qualifying competition of the 1896/97 Amateur Cup. The FA, though, soon reverted to type when the Amateur Cup semi-finalists received their shares of the gates. RA were awarded the lowest sum of £6 18s, while their defeated opponents Shrewsbury benefited by £14 19s 1d. This was slightly more than the £14 15s 6d received by Darlington, while the highest amount of £43 2s 6d went to the cup's winners, Bishop Auckland.

But further confirmation of RA's growing status came with the close season acceptance of their application to become members of the Hampshire FA. This was followed by their admittance to membership of the Football Association as the 1896/97 campaign began.

Improvements were carried out at the US Men's Ground for the new season to give better facilities for the thousands of spectators who regularly turned up for RA's home games. The old stand was roofed with zinc and a new stand was built on the opposite touchline. The refurbishment would add greatly to the comfort of fans, according to press reports.

The supporters were expected to attend in greater numbers with the formation of the Hampshire Senior League. The prospect of the new competition excited the *Portsmouth Evening News* as RA faced up to their first regular set of fixtures. The league initially consisted of eight clubs. RA were the only representatives from eastern Hampshire. Their opponents were St Mary's Reserves, Freemantle, Eastleigh, Cowes, Ryde, Bournemouth, and Andover. 'The league programme promises some exciting matches,' wrote the newspaper:

'and some of the clubs engaged will be greatly benefited from the interest which will accrue from the fixtures being league ones. Most of the clubs are up to the strength of London Senior Cup clubs. St Mary's Reserves have a few professional players and will be very strong. Their matches with RA, Cowes and Freemantle are sure to be thrilling.'

Meanwhile, the emerging Southern League was set to be one of the best outside the Football League. Some of its members, such as RA's rivals Southampton St Mary's, were joining the growing ranks of professional outfits. The Southern League was one of the few competitions RA would not seemingly be competing in.

Sgt Bonney, described as an energetic and genial secretary, needed those qualities in abundance to keep up with The Gunners' progress in the English, Army, Amateur, Hampshire Senior and Portsmouth Senior Cups along with the new Hampshire Senior League. The reserves were taking part in the Hampshire Junior Cup.

The days of appealing for friendly opponents to fill vacant Saturdays were over as the organization of football around Portsmouth stepped up a gear. As a spectacle it was an exciting one, the *Portsmouth Evening News* decided, and would cheer all of the town's footballers who took an interest in RA:

'The prospects of success remain to be seen but, as there will not be many changes in the team, nearly all of last season's men being able to appear in their usual places, the outlook seems very rosy.'

The Hampshire Telegraph backed that view. The newspaper put RA among the five clubs capable of winning the inaugural Hampshire Senior League title. The other contenders were St Mary's Reserves, Freemantle, Cowes and Eastleigh. It wrote:

'…the Artillery having a splendid pick of men, while the civilian clubs are all stiffening their teams by enlisting the services of professionals.'

For the *Portsmouth Times*, RA had real chances of lifting a haul of trophies:

'Great hopes are centred upon this season… and great disappointment will be felt if they don't bag two or three of the trophies. They will fortunately be able to rely on the same team which did so well last season.'

But the reporter at the *Southern Daily Mail*, the new title of *The Mail* (Portsmouth), accused The Gunners of failing to learn the lessons of the previous campaign:

'Of the RA at present, I have not heard a lot, except that they have entered for every competition for which they were qualified – possibly on the principle that if you try for the lot you may get something. Overwork probably cost them the Amateur and Portsmouth Senior cups last season but their executive, far from profiting by the loss, have arranged a bigger programme than ever. All the old men are, I hear, available but I certainly think the side are attempting too much. But, anyhow, good luck to them. They won't give anything away for want of trying.'

Of the Portsmouth Senior Cup-holders 15th Co RA, there was bad news in the *Southern Daily Mail* rather than negative comments:

'I am sorry to say I do not hear very flourishing accounts of the team. Scattered indeed are the famous band who went from victory to victory seasons ago. Cook, McDonald and Harper were with the RA last season, McKie with the Saints, Brownlie at Freemantle and Jackson at Eastleigh, where Moorhouse joined him early in October.'

The lack of players ruled out entry for the 15th Co RA to join RA in the Hampshire Senior League, though several cups were to be contested. But while The Gunners were established as Portsmouth's foremost military side, plenty of other sides of soldiers made the town a flourishing soccer scene for the service. The 4th Co RA shared Cambridge Barracks with The Gunners, while the 20th Co RA, Hilsea RA, 34th Co Portsmouth and 20th Co Fareham also fielded sides.

RA heralded a campaign which was to continue their meteoric progress by duly beating their reserves in a practice match at the US Men's Ground as well as RMA 6–0 in a friendly.

But controversy soon surfaced. An eight-goal thrashing of Andover got RA's Hampshire Senior League life off to the best possible start on September 26 with their biggest win in the league to confirm the newspapers' general optimism.

Heavy rain made play difficult and RA were reported to be below their usual form, which must have worried their forthcoming opponents. They piled on the pressure from the start, however, with Reilly playing in the unaccustomed position of left-back and Walsh netting four goals to lead the way in front of goal.

Some fans, though, among those who ensured the new stand was well patronized were angry at the performance of the referee, Mr C.D. Crisp, in spite of the runaway victory. RA were 8–0 up, and still pressing, when the abuse began of Mr Crisp, the honorary secretary of the Portsmouth and District Referees' Association.

He answered the loudmouths and got the worst of the argument. He later explained the slanging match as arising from an insulting remark from one spectator. He stopped the game and protested to the man, who apologized. While this episode continued, Mr Crisp said, there were generous cheers for him from other spectators.

Perhaps of more lasting interest to RA's fans was the experiment of playing Reilly in an outfield position. *The Portsmouth Evening News* reporter was unimpressed by the tactical change:

> *'Reilly did not come out of the ordeal very well for, though he could kick well enough and his weight stood him in good stead, he seemed rather lost and not at home in his new position. It must be remembered, however, it is two years since Reilly played at back. He was possibly not too sure out of goal as in it, where he is one of the finest keepers in the army.'*

Other rare team news to emerge from the season's early weeks concerned the fact half-back Hogg and centre-half Kinman would not be playing. Hogg's place was taken by McKenzie. RA's increasing status off the field was shown by the publication at the end of September of their first fixture list. The production, said to be neat and convenient, had a blue cover with the club's crest in gilt on the front. It was completed by a pencil attached to the front.

That growing role was reflected in the receipts from the opening game. They totalled £17, more than had been taken at previous Portsmouth Senior Cup finals. The amount was easily topped by the £39 paid by the near 3,000 fans at the home Hampshire Senior League game with Eastleigh a week later as an argument raged in Portsmouth's footballing circles about the wisdom of allowing RA to monopolise all the set quota of matches at the Men's Ground for which admission had to be paid.

But as the Artillerymen went from strength to strength, 15th Co RA were facing a severe blow. An announcement in the *Portsmouth Times* in late September heralded the end of the club as a footballing force:

> *'Much regret will be felt by footballers in the district at the announcement that the 15th Co RA (holders of the Portsmouth and Artillery cups), now stationed at Fort Grange, have been ordered to proceed to Malta.'*

15th Co managed to stagger on for two more years on the football pitch as a mere shadow of their former selves. October began for RA with that lucrative early season, top-of-the-table Hampshire Senior League clash with Eastleigh, a place below first-placed RA. The Gunners recorded their second win in two games. A brace of goals from Cook and another by Walsh gave them a 3–0 victory and the record of:

P2 W2 D0 L0 F11 A0 Pts 4.

LOCAL MATCHES.

HAMPSHIRE LEAGUE.

ROYAL ARTILLERY v. EASTLEIGH.—The Artillery team fulfilled their second engagement in the Hampshire League this afternoon, the match with Eastleigh attracting fully 2,000 spectators, who cheered the teams as they lined out at 3.30 as under:—

Royal Artillery: Goal, Gunner Reilly; backs, Corporal Harms and Gunner Phillips; half-backs, Gunner McKenzie, Gunner Hill, and Gunner Hogg; forwards, Bombardier Meggs and Corporal Welsh, right; Bombardier Hanna, centre; Gunner Jardine and Gunner Cook, left wing.

Eastleigh — Goal, Collins; backs, Brockiehurst and Dexter; half-backs, Lawless, Hillyard, and Shearman; forwards, Sharpe and Jackson, right wing; Woodhouse, centre; Bostock and Jeffcoat, left wing.

Referee, Mr. McLaughlin, Southampton.

The principal change in the arrangement of the home team since the meeting with Andover last week was the return of Reilly to his old place in goal, Jackson making his first appearance on the Eastleigh side against his old comrades. The turf was firmer than last Saturday, the weather fine though dull, and there was every prospect of an interesting game. Some minutes were lost in waiting for the referee, but a start was made at 5.45, when the home team kicked off. They had to yield to a fierce attack but a foul given against them looked awkward but was smartly met, and the civilians had to defend their goal, but were smart upon the ball, and after some

RA's second home fixture in the Hampshire Senior League as reported by the Southern Daily Mail.

The teams met again a week later in the English Cup's preliminary round. Eastleigh proved the pre-match predictions wrong when they held RA to a 1–1 draw after 90 minutes in another game touched by controversy. The Gunners seemed well on their way to a repeat win when they took the lead just before the end of the first quarter of extra-time. A piece of direct play saw Reilly kick the ball to the halfway line. Meggs ran through and scored. But it was not enough to secure a place in the next round. Mr Whittaker, the referee, abandoned the game with just a few minutes to go because of the fading light.

RA used their understandable annoyance to good effect with a convincing 7–1 win in the replay in Portsmouth the following week but they had to come from a goal behind after the visitors had taken the lead from a goalmouth scramble.

The Gunners had been expected to go through to the next round but in a more modest fashion, according to the *Portsmouth Evening News*:

'The convincing win must have come as a surprise to even the most strenuous believer in the local team. Play in the first-half was not extraordinary in its result but the way in which after the interval RA bottled up the Eastleigh defence was quite unexpected.'

The visitors contained three 15th Co RA players, along with two ex-soldiers, but none could match Meggs's impact. The newspaper reported he made the afternoon's most effective shot in taking a second-half penalty:

'He never misses a shot of that kind and one rather pities the keeper who has to wait for the ball which lands plump in his net as if a charge of powder was behind it…'

It was another aspect of The Gunners vigorous play which concerned the *Southern Daily Mail*'s reporter, "A.N. Other":

'I would advise certain members of the team, who shall be nameless, to exercise more self-control otherwise I believe there may be trouble. I don't believe these players are intentionally rough but their natural over-eagerness and anxiety to excess should be curbed. One does not like to see certain referees continually hauling up the same players, and an abundance of free kicks for fouls causes much unpleasantness not only for the players but more particularly amongst the spectators.'

Meggs was on the scoresheet again as RA kept their Hampshire Senior League clean sheet intact with a 4–0 victory in their first league away fixture, at Bournemouth. The Gunners were superior in all positions. Only erratic shooting kept their score down. RA, meanwhile, sought and received permission from the FA to bring forward their second preliminary round tie in the English Cup away to Oxford Cygnets a week to October 24. The game was noticeable for the first mention, Army Cup final aside, of train tickets on sale from RA for 9s 4d to watch the team in action. They proved money well spent for any fans who made the long journey.

The Cygnets' half-backs, all of them with county caps, could not stop Meggs putting The Gunners a goal up inside the opening two minutes. They held on to the lead in spite of a fightback by the home side. The 3–1 extra time victory put RA into the cup's qualifying competition after three matches in two rounds. The qualifiers comprised a further four rounds before the competition proper began with the entry of the professional clubs.

RA's opponents on their way to a possible clash with a top side were to be Eastville Rovers or Bristol St George's. RA had the choice of ground. The draw delighted the club. Arch-rivals and leading Hampshire club Southampton St Mary's had been avoided to give The Gunners every chance of getting through.

St George's had lost 3–2 to 15th Co RA a year earlier but were reckoned to be stronger than their Western League rivals of Eastville Rovers. All three of St George's games had ended in wins, while Rovers had only two points from a solitary win in their opening four matches.

Before the Bristol sides met to decide which would face RA, the club had another fine honour bestowed upon them. They were to supply more than half the army's team for a match against the celebrated London Corinthians. RA's officials were highly delighted by the official recognition for the annual fixture with a side which supplied the entire England team twice in the 1890s and whose name was renowned for high playing ideals and giant-killing.

Of the seven RA players chosen, and the six who turned out, Reilly inevitably gained the plaudits in the army's 4–1 defeat. The past three seasons had seen The Corinthians win 11–1, 8–1 and 10–0. Superb was a word often used to describe Reilly's performance in the match. His saves and clearances kept the servicemen's hopes alive.

Bombardier John Hanna, RA's captain, who led the team to three Army Cup finals in four seasons.

The Athletic News said he was good enough for any team if his display in the game was his true form. Walsh had one or two good chances on the right wing and Hanna played well in place of the injured Cook at centre-forward, despite missing several openings. Phillips also put in some serviceable tackles, though it was recognised the Corinthians put out a weakened team compared to previous years. RA's other representatives were Jardine and Meggs.

All six players were in the RA side which started the quest for the 1896/97 Army Cup with a 3–1 first round win over Royal Sussex Regiment. On another cup front, two days later, RA had been selected for a preliminary round tie with HMS Vernon in the Portsmouth Senior Cup. The largest-ever entry of 18 clubs meant two preliminary games were needed. The Artillerymen came through theirs 9–0 on the last day of October.

Tyre turned a rare outing in the first team into a personal triumph by scoring eight of the goals. It was both a record team and individual performance. The left-winger opened the scoring after 15 minutes in which play had all been in Vernon's half. Doyle added a second goal before Tyre began to dominate proceedings with a third. Soon after the re-start, Vernon stepped up a gear in vain as Tyre continued to find the net. His third, and RA's fourth, came straight after the kick-off. And he just continued scoring. In a masterly piece of understatement, the *Southern Daily Mail* said of Tyre's display:

'*In midfield he is not much of a player, but he can shoot.*'

The result was bettered within a fortnight as RA notched up a record 15-0 win against hapless Dublin Fusiliers in the cup's first round. RA were eight goals up at half-time and some of the team were not even on the pitch as the second-half got underway.

The goals were spread around. Hanna scored five, Walsh and Meggs notched a hat-trick apiece, Cook two and Jardine and Harms one each. Tyre, the hero of the previous round, was missing from the team. The result earned The Gunners a second round outing against old foes RMLI and ensured they lived up to two complimentary press articles. Both were about their star goalkeeper, of course.

Athletic News was the first to sing Reilly's praises:

'RA head the Hampshire Senior League with a 15–0 goal average, thanks to Reilly, who is far and away the most resourceful keeper the army has ever had.'

The Regiment followed a day later with an unflattering response to a request from Arsenal for the keeper:

'We believe Gnr Reilly was recently approached by Woolwich Arsenal FC with a view to him playing a vital game. Considering the Artilleryman's ability between the sticks has won him previously tempting offers from many First Division league clubs the request from the Arsenal people savours a style of that display of cool effrontery which Tommy Atkins terms a "hard neck".'

The Southern Daily Mail added its opinion to the value of Reilly in helping his team to a 100 per cent record by mid-November. "A.N. Other" wrote:

'A rumour reaches me that a certain first league club – to wit Stoke – are exceedingly anxious to secure Reilly and have practically asked him to name his terms. For his own sake, I hope he will not abandon the artillery for the precarious paths of professionalism.'

Such plaudits for RA's star keeper were enough to scare off their intended opponents in the third qualifying round of the English Cup. The week after their 15–0 victory over Dublin Fusiliers, they should have faced Eastville Rovers. But the Bristol side kept up that city's tradition for pulling out of matches with The Gunners by instead turning out in the Western League against neighbours Warmley. *The Western Daily Press* made clear the reason for the change:

'As Eastville Rovers were drawn to meet RA at Portsmouth and their chances of success were remote, they scratched…'

Sergeant Williams scored one of the two second-half goals in RA's first match. But the outside-right, who played at No 9 in that debut game, featured only fitfully in the early seasons.

November 1896 – April 1897
The Invincibles

November ended with RA confirming their growing reputation by winning a game which press previews said would be the most exciting in Portsmouth in 1896. A 30th minute Harms free-kick out on the right struck Everett, an East Lancashire Regiment back, to settle a Hampshire Senior Cup second round tie between the sides in front of a large crowd of nearly 5,000 at the Men's Ground. The match lived up to its billing, with the East Lancs top of the Aldershot League with seven wins from seven games. *The Portsmouth Evening News* commented:

> '*A lot of money changed hands over RA's victory on Saturday but those who backed the East Lancashires have at least the satisfaction of knowing the team of their choice made a great fight. The only goal in the game showed no weakness on the visitors' part, though The Gunners ought to have scored several times and would have done so but for the ball, ducking away to the wind, playing false. Meggs, especially, had no luck. RA certainly played their best game and it was a pity they did not win by a higher margin.*'

Back in the Hampshire Senior League, another emphatic victory allowed RA to regain the top spot taken by Cowes while The Gunners were on cup duty. Ryde were RA's latest victims and 7–0 was the score. Unusually, seven players netted a goal each to keep up The Gunners' 100 per cent record from their four league fixtures.

Their nickname of The Invincibles was being lived up to but their success was again causing them to run out of Saturdays on which to arrange fixtures. RMLI were the unhappy victims of RA's success for the second season in a row. The teams had been due to meet in the Portsmouth Senior Cup on the day RA were set to play Swindon Town away in another of the English Cup's qualifying rounds.

Portsmouth FA officials sympathised with RA's predicament. They agreed the club had done more than any other for the game in the town and decided to delay the local tie in spite of strong protests by RMLI, though The Gunners' fixture congestion was eased in an unfortunate way when their interest in the English Cup came to an end at a soggy Swindon with a 4–1 defeat.

The home side had been thought to provide an easier fixture than Reading, RA's other possible opponents, but the Wiltshire team were thoroughly at home in the miserable conditions on the day. Reilly had kept RA in the game with the half-time score at 0–0 but Swindon took advantage of a change of clothes during the interval and played the second-half comparatively warm and dry.

RA, by contrast, could do nothing to cheer themselves up but they could console themselves with the thought they played the best the circumstances allowed. It was their first defeat after 11 straight wins. Yet, as one cup competition ended for RA, another began.

Having been exempt from the Amateur Cup's preliminary competition after reaching the previous season's final, they were drawn against Old Etonians in the first round proper. Before that, however, the year came to a close as it traditionally did with the fixture between the football associations of Brighton and Portsmouth. RA provided seven members of the Portsmouth side.

The club's ranks were boosted in early 1897 with the transfer of Sgt Coleman from Sheerness to the RA's Cambridge Barracks headquarters. A well-known player in Kent, Coleman had played for the county team and regularly turned out for Sheppey United in the Southern League's first division. He would be an asset to RA, the *Portsmouth Evening News* reckoned, with a good reputation and being a noted sprinter. However, he was absent when his new team lost their 100 per cent Hampshire Senior League record in a top-of-the-table clash with Cowes in front of some 3,000 spectators at the US Men's Ground on the second day of 1897.

Both teams stayed unbeaten but Cowes had to be the happier side with the 2–2 result. Walsh and Jardine had hauled RA backed into the game after the visitors had twice gone in front as The Gunners conceded their first goals in the league.

The sides resumed their rivalry a month afterwards in the semi-finals of the Hampshire Senior Cup, with Cowes winning by the game's only goal. It was the game's atmosphere rather than its result which occupied the *Southern Daily Mail* of February 13:

> *'Hard knocks were given and taken and the match was by no means a pleasant one. The Cowes "sportsmen" hooted the Artillerymen as soon as they appeared on the ground and generally comported themselves in the way for which they are famous, or rather notorious, in their island home.'*

A few months later would see the sides engaged in another battle. But a further cup tie for RA, with RMLI in the Portsmouth Senior Cup, was scratched by the opponents who had gone to great lengths a few weeks earlier to be so awkward about the arrangements. RA were unperturbed and went back to winning ways with a 5–1 Hampshire Senior League defeat of Ryde. A visit to Freemantle kept them top of the league and undefeated after seven games even though a draw meant a point dropped.

RA's continued success was again recognized by the army. Four players turned out for the service's fixture with a London XI on January 21. They were Harms (back), Walsh, Meggs and new recruit Coleman (forwards). All played well and Coleman, who had taken Hanna's place after the initial squad selection, scored the army's goal in a narrow victory.

But the Artillerymen's growing stature laid behind talks held between the FA and its army counterpart to determine the vexed status of military footballers. The subject left them with nothing to fear, in the eyes of the *Southern Daily Mail*. They were soldiers first and footballers second, "A.N. Other" declared.

Snow caused RA's Portsmouth Senior Cup semi-final at the US Men's Ground with the Army Service Corps to be postponed. Drifts on the pitch were a foot deep in places and the ground underneath was frozen hard. The re-arranged fixture at the start of February was well worth the wait for RA fans. They saw their team romp to a 15–0 win to equal their record victory in their previous game in the cup.

A less spectacular, but equally satisfying, triumph saw RA into the Amateur Cup's second round when they eased past Old Etonians 3–2 at Leyton. A three-goal first half burst put RA well in charge and they resisted the Etonians' late efforts. Again, though, The Gunners skirted controversy as they apparently played to the verge of sportsmanship. Their tactics upset some national commentators: 'Their football was of the severe type and one or two of the forwards are possessed of manners that would put Red Indians to the blush or their equivalent,' trumpeted the *Morning Leader*.

The Daily Chronicle added its condemnatory voice: 'Few professional teams could have given as unworthy a display as the winners of this tie.' Yet "A.N. Other" was clear what The Gunners' real crime had been:

'Possibly winning the match was the greatest offence the RA committed in the eyes of the London population at any rate.' But the reason for the antagonism could have laid in an incident two years previously. Old Etonians were then drawn against another military side from Portsmouth, King's Own Lancasters, in the Amateur Cup. The tie failed to take place owing to a 'misunderstanding', to use the *Southern Daily Mail*'s description, and the regiment walked into the semi-final: 'There was a great deal of unpleasantness over it at the time, and the sides laid their versions of the event before the public through the sporting press,' the newspaper continued.

The win pitched The Gunners against Casuals at Tufnell Park. This time, the Portsmouth side were on the wrong end of a 3–2 scoreline on February 13 to a club who had been finalists in the first Amateur Cup competition in 1894. There was better news in the third round of the Army Cup as RA defeated RA Gosport 3–0.

A goal difference of 34–4 from just eight games kept The Gunners top of the Hampshire Senior League as March began over rivals who had played more games. A 6–0 win at Andover, in which Cook scored a hat-trick in the opening 15 minutes, reinforced that fine record.

But it came at a personal cost for two Artillerymen. Hill (24) and Phillips (26) appeared in court two days after the March 6 game because of a post-match celebration that went too far. Hill was found guilty of being drunk and disorderly and assaulting a policeman in Commercial Road.

It needed four or five officers to take him into custody after a violent struggle. He was fined 20s including costs or seven days in prison. Phillips was fined 10s including costs or five days in prison for being drunk and disorderly in the disturbance.

Back on the pitch, plenty of goals were also in evidence as RA triumphed 6–1 away to the King's Own Lancashire Regiment at Plymouth in the Army Cup's fourth round. The next game The Gunners played in the

Gunner Davie Phillips - one of The Gunners' most consistent players, appearing 117 times.

competition was also given as being in the fourth round in press reports.

What was not in doubt was the identity of the opponents who would face RA in the next round. The East Lancashires awaited them again and revenge was on the mind of The Lilywhites for the single-goal defeat they suffered at the hands of RA in the Hampshire Senior Cup. The Aldershot-based outfit engaged a trainer from Burnley for the latest clash. He was expected to instil some of the methods which the famous club had used since being a founder member of the Football League.

RA were taking their training seriously as well, under Hanna's guidance, and engaged in running and kicking sessions at the Men's Ground. Club secretary Sgt Bonney arranged an excursion for the large amount of local interest in the fixture. Those among the 7,000 crowd who made the journey to Aldershot watched RA go through with another 1–0 win, after an exciting tussle, to a semi-final pairing with 3rd Grenadier Guards at the beginning of April.

Before then, RA had consolidated their top spot in the Hampshire Senior League against a St Mary's Reserves side specially strengthened with several first team players to stave off a repeat of the 4–0 defeat at the hands of The Gunners earlier in the season. They only succeeded in narrowing the margin of defeat in the fixture on March 24 to three goals. Two more league fixtures – both won – saw RA work through their backlog of games and stay in first place, but their thoughts were preoccupied with the Army Cup semi-final.

3rd Grenadier Guards had proved spirited opponents the previous season when they had only been defeated by RA in the Amateur Cup at the third attempt. They lived up to expectations in the latest clash, holding RA to a 1–1 draw after extra time at the County Ground at Southampton. The Guards had the best of the opening 45 minutes. Reilly had a couple of narrow escapes. One shot hit his right-hand post.

The tempo of play hotted up after the interval and RA took the lead amid scenes of great excitement. Harms played a free-kick into the goalmouth at just the right height. It touched one of a crowd of players, no one could see who, and cannoned into the net. The Guards drew level ten minutes later from a penalty after Phillips played a goalbound shot on to his hands.

Reilly reached Robertson's spot-kick but, despite this, the wet and greasy ball slipped through his grasp into the net. Extra time was quiet as both of the evenly-matched sides tired. Reilly was his side's saviour once again with his brilliant stops. He was joined as RA's man of the match by Kinman. A repeat of the previous season's three encounters between the sides looked possible.

But RA's 2–1 replay win ruled out the need for a further meeting. Nine carriages of supporters made the midweek journey to Guildford, again, on a special train to see another unknown scorer put The Gunners through to their second Army Cup final in three seasons and a third for Reilly, Hanna and Harms.

The Gunners did most of the attacking in a goalless first-half and there could be no dispute about the name of the player who gave them the lead 17 minutes after the interval. Meggs beat the Guards' keeper, Rafter, from a pass by Coleman.

Their opponents drew level through Molyneaux with a shot which Reilly, with the sun in his eyes, was unable to see. As the excitement mounted in the closing minutes RA won a string of corners. Jardine sent in a good kick which one of several players in the goalmouth headed in. The Gunners held on to win to face the Lancashire Fusiliers in the final just five days later.

April 1897
Army Cup Winners Again

Arrangements were quickly made to take a thousand spectators to Aldershot to swell the crowd for the Easter Monday highlight of the military soccer season to 15,000. RA lined up taller and heavier than the opposition as they looked to continue their winning form. A pre-match line-up gave the teams' vital statistics as follows:

RA:
Gunner Reilly – 5ft 11½in 13st 4lb;
Corporal Harms – 5ft 11½in 12st;
Gnr Phillips – 5ft 9in 13st;
Gnr Kinman 5ft 10¾in 12st 4lb;
Cpl Hanna (cpt) – 5ft 9in 12st;
Gnr Hill 5ft 9in 12st 12lb;
Bombardier Meggs 5ft 8in 12st 5lb;
Cpl Walsh 5ft 9½in 12st;
Gnr Cook 5ft 9in 11st 4lb;
Sergeant Coleman 5ft 8in 11st 11lb;
Gnr Jardine 5ft 8in 11st 12lb.

Lancashire Fusiliers:
Musician Simpson – 5ft 10½in 12st;
Lance-Corporal Taylor – 5ft 7¾in 12st 4lb;
L-Cpl Durham – 5ft 8in 11st 4lb;
Msc Sewell – 5ft 6in 8st 3lb;
Msc Rhodes – 5ft 7½in 11st 6lb;
Private Simmons – 5ft 5¼in 9st 4lb;
Pvt Howarth – 5ft 4½in 10st 6lb;
Pvt Simmons – 5ft 4½in 10st 6lb;
Pvt Walsh – 5ft 7¼in 9st 6lb;
L-Cpl Small – 5ft 7in 10st;
Pvt Banks 5ft 7in 10st 2lb.

It seemed as if The Gunners' hopes had taken a knock in the early minutes when they were reduced to nine men. Coleman was practically disabled by a nasty kick and the forward was joined on the injured list by his captain, Hanna, with a twisted right knee. RA battled to overcome this lack of numbers and Harms's well-judged free-kick was headed home by left-winger Jardine to great cheers from the RA fans.

Fifteen minutes were left and Reilly had to show amazing alertness when he fisted the ball out twice in quick succession as the Fusiliers mounted an exciting struggle to draw level. They were kept at bay as play in the closing stages became more even to ensure the injured Hanna received the cup from HRH The Duchess of Connaught.

The victorious team and their fans returned to Portsmouth in two long trains. They were greeted inside the town station by tumultuous scenes with several hundred well-wishers crowding the platforms and the RA band playing "See The Conquering Hero Comes" once more. Harms, so instrumental in the win, was carried on the crowd's shoulders with the cup into the wet streets.

The players moved off in a large open wagonette to the Cambridge Barracks to celebrate their latest crowning as the best team in the army. Twice in three years they had won the Army Cup. The previous season's semi-final defeat by the Royal Scots was their only setback in 21 matches which stretched back three years. They had truly made the competition their own.

A hat-trick from Gunner David Jardine played a large part in the only Portsmouth Senior Cup success enjoyed by RA. The outside-left achieved the feat of the only hat-trick scored by a gunner in a final when they played Southsea Rovers on March 20, 1897.

The cup was also the second piece of silverware The Gunners had won in three weeks following an ill-tempered 5–0 roasting of Southsea Rovers in the Portsmouth Senior Cup final. Referee Mr C.D. Crisp, involved in a similarly controversial occasion with The Gunners at the season's start, had to call together all the players in the middle of the pitch to tell them to cool their tempers after a series of fouls.

Everyone but Reilly joined the lecture. In typically headstrong mood, the keeper would not budge from his goal. When the fouls stopped, and the football began, goals from Hanna, Meggs and Jardine (2) gave RA a convincing half time lead. Jardine completed his hat-trick after the interval in front of a packed ground.

RA's first fixture after their Army Cup triumph was a charity match with the 2nd Gordon Highlanders. It raised £31 6s 3d for military charities. RA fielded most of the cup winners, with the injured Hanna and Coleman absent, in losing 2–0.

The two casualties were still missing when RA took on Cowes in a Hampshire Senior League title decider on April 24 at the Brooklyn Ground on the Isle of Wight. The home team secured the championship with a goal from a free-kick scored by McCrindle or E. Baker, depending on which match report was read, just before half-time.

But the occasion was overshadowed, once again, by an uproar. The Cowes supporters rioted after Harms had disabled home forward F. Moore in the first-half by kneeing him in the chest by his heart – twice!! The Cowes player was felled after the second incident and was finished for the rest of the game.

He was forced to retire to the dressing room as the home supporters hurled abuse at Harms. The back escaped punishment by the referee but he needed the protection of the police to escape punishment by the crowd. Harms had a warm reception, as the *Isle of Wight County Press* described the situation, as he left the pitch at half-time: 'A crowd gathering round him in a threatening kind of way,' the newspaper reported.

That was merely a prelude to the after-match reception which awaited the gunner. Retribution was on the crowd's mind, instead of celebration, at Cowes' single-goal victory after Hamnett in the home goal had foiled all of RA's attacks to clinch the league title from their nearest challengers. *The Isle of Wight County Press* seemed almost joyful in its account of the mayhem:

'After the match, Harms appears to have had a very warm time of it. He was followed by a jeering crowd and pelted with orange peel, and would have no doubt undergone rougher treatment had it not been for the protection of the police who conducted him to the bridge leading across the railway line in Terminus Road. There he crossed and escaped, while the constables held back his pursuers. He eventually got to the Salterns stage where the gunboat was waiting to take him and the rest of the RA back to Portsmouth, and thus he got away safely.'

The Portsmouth Times of May 1 was clear about who was to blame for the riotous behaviour:

'Cowes supporters do not bear a very good character and the disgraceful way in which they treated the RA on Saturday will not improve their reputation. The Gunners were continually hooted and hissed, and on the way to the boat, they were almost mobbed. I hear of a possible protest and, if this is true, I hope the Artillery will get it.'

The fixture had a history of unsavoury incidents. Among them was the match between Cowes and RA (Fort Rowner, Gosport) in April 1894 which descended into chaos. The flashpoint arose after Cowes had gone into the lead with two second-half goals.

Referee Mr C.D. Crisp, once more, rebuked one of the Artillerymen for swearing. The captain of the military team, who was unnamed in the newspaper report, made a remark to Mr Crisp, who ordered him off. He walked off the pitch accompanied by several of his team-mates. The mass disruption brought the game to an end, with Cowes 2–1 ahead.

RA's officials were, indeed, angry about events in the 1897 game. Treasurer and trainer RSM Fred Windrum alleged he had been hit on the head with a brick thrown by a Cowes supporter. He told a council meeting of the Hampshire FA a riot would have broken out if RA had taken 200/300 fans across the Solent. RA's adjutant-general also sent a formal letter of complaint about the incidents.

An inquiry was set up by the association after its chairman, Mr C.G. Ellarby, mentioned serious trouble had affected the Cowes *v* Ryde derby game earlier in the season. Mr Ellarby was joined on the inquiry team by the FA's honorary secretary, Mr Pickford, and a Mr T.E. Brutt. The Cowes representative at the meeting, Mr Wall, said the club would co-operate with the association's investigations.

The inquiry fully backed RA's complaints when it reported a month later. The panel decided some Cowes spectators behaved in a disorderly manner at the ground. At half-time, the home club had been forced to step up precautions after missiles were thrown at The Gunners.

But the efforts were inadequate to stop a hostile demonstration against RA's players outside the ground after the match, though the team had ignored a request to leave by another exit. The committee ordered Cowes to apologise to RA for the conduct of their supporters and imposed two sanctions on the offenders.

A minimum admission fee of 1s was ordered for all home games the following September and October and warnings from the Hampshire FA had to be displayed conspicuously around the ground. Dr Hoffmeister, of Cowes, blamed RA for all the trouble but the island club accepted the committee's verdict as being designed to hit the guilty people rather than the club.

Cowes were still Hampshire Senior League champions, whatever the inquiry's deliberations. RA's league season had petered out with a 3–3 draw against Eastleigh. The fixture, originally due to have been played away, had to be re-arranged several times before it finally took place on April 28. The delay meant The Gunners were forced to use Governor's Green at Old Portsmouth after they were refused permission to play at the Men's Ground.

The Eastleigh game completed, RA finished runners-up to Cowes. The defeat amid the stormy scenes at Cowes was their sole setback in a league game through a season in which the Artillerymen's goalscoring reached a peak.

Their record of: P14 W10 D3 L1 F54 A8 Pts 23

compared well to that of Cowes: P14 W11 D3 L0 F45 A10 Pts 25.

But it was not enough to win the title or, seemingly, take the next step up the football ladder by entering the Southern League.

Hampshire Senior League 1896/97

	P	W	D	L	F	A	Pts
Cowes	14	11	3	0	45	10	25
Royal Artillery (Portsmouth)	14	10	3	1	54	8	23
Freemantle	14	9	1	4	28	19	19
Eastleigh Athletic	14	4	5	5	43	39	13
Southampton St Mary's Res	14	3	5	6	20	23	11
Bournemouth	14	4	1	9	16	50	9
Andover	14	3	2	9	16	45	8
Ryde	14	1	2	11	10	47	4

Summer – December 1897
Into the Southern League

May's annual meeting of the Southern League rejected RA's bid to join, along with Eastleigh, in favour of St Alban's. RA did have some good news with which to console themselves in the close season. They had again been exempted from the FA Cup's qualifying rounds. They were in illustrious company. Reading, Southampton, St Mary's and Swindon Town were similarly excused. Two months later, there was even better news for 1897/98. RA, as well as continuing in the Hampshire Senior League, were members of the Southern League's second division.

The resignation of Freemantle created a vacancy in the 12-strong division and the loss of the team which had finished third the previous season was amply filled by one which was a mere four years old. The promotion was warmly, if cautiously, greeted by the *Portsmouth Evening News*:

> *'RA have done so much for local football. They deserve their congratulations on their promotion. It's to be hoped they will not be overwhelmed in the coming season. This new league, as well as the Hampshire Seenior League and cup competitions, means a lot of travelling. The RA fixture card will, says Sgt Bonney have 38 league matches on it, which will be plenty to keep them occupied during cup games.'*

One Player not taking part in any more RA games was Cook. He was signed by Eastleigh to strengthen their forwards upon their acceptance into the Western League after having been rejected by the Southern League. Cook joined another ex-RA player McDonald to form Eastleigh's left wing. On the other flank, Knox, a further one-time Gunner, completed their RA connections. As August began, RA's thoughts were with the Hampshire Senior League's old season rather than the competitions approaching campaign in which they would be joined by Cowes, Freemantle, Andover, Bournemouth, Ryde and St Mary's Reserves as well as Eastleigh. The object of their attention was that turbulent championship decider at Cowes.

Mr Matthews, one of the island club's three representatives at the Hampshire FA's annual meeting, told delegates the club wanted the matter reconsidered and the prohibitive admission charge of 1s removed. Cowes were more than £100 in debt and in a state of bankruptcy, he said. The outfit had taken every step it could to prevent a repeat of the riotous events and had arranged that no undesirable persons should be admitted.

They had apologized to RA, as ordered, and the army club was willing for the matter to be discussed again. RA secretary Sgt Bonney

Sergeant Richard Bonney, RA's ever-loyal and hard-working secretary.

emphasised the reconciliation when he seconded the proposal and the meeting approved a motion which called on the Hampshire FA council to look again at Cowes' admission charge. The move was supported by the council when it met a few weeks later.

The overwhelming spirit of the footballing times was to look forward rather than back. This was shown by the formation of a new league, backed by the *Hampshire Telegraph*, for service teams in Portsmouth. The United Services League was to consist of up to 12 members. They would be the pick of the service clubs, with RA Reserves representing the town's premier outfit whose success had laid the foundations for the new set-up. It would be augmented by a cup competition, with a trophy paid for by the newspaper.

The scale of the challenge taken on by RA's first team for 1897/98 could be seen at the end of August when the club's fixture list was issued for a footballing world whose speed of progress was gauged by events at two of the club's long-standing rivals. Southampton St Mary's had become Southampton, reformed into a limited company to match their professional status of three years, and were planning a move to The Dell. Bristol South End had just turned pro and also shortened their name to Bristol City.

No such alterations were possible at the strictly military RA but the club could gain some consolation by being able to prove their equal to anything to be found among their Southern League rivals of Dartford, Southall and Maidenhead in the league's second division. The Gunners kept most of their familiar squad. Their captain for the exciting eight months in prospect – Sgt Hanna – proved the strong thread of continuity which ran through The Gunners' preparations. His vice-captain was the team's star keeper, Gnr Reilly. A 21-strong squad was registered for the Hampshire League and their identities were beginning to become more publicly known in spite of Victorian formality. The players were: Harms, Hill, Fletcher, Coutts, Jardine, McNeil, Phillips, Kinman, Reilly, Coleman, Tyre, Haxton, Hanna, Phinn, Pitt, Walsh, Patterson, Meggs, McCabe, Field, and Maxwell.

The appearance of Phillips in the list disproved rumours he was set to leave The Gunners. But Meggs and Patterson were reported to be doubtful for the season ahead. Meggs was likely to miss all the campaign because of seriously infected eyes, while Patterson was in hospital with an abscess on his face.

The growth in RA's activities meant Sgt Bonney, as energetic and hard-working as he was, needed help in his secretarial duties for the first time in the form of QMS W.J. Manley. RSM Windrum stayed as honorary treasurer and trainer.

RA's first outing of the season, at the start of September, was the same as in previous years with a practice match against the reserves. The reserves won 2–1, though the teams were more mixed than their names implied. But one aspect of the 1897/98 season was different from those that had gone before. RA had not entered for the Amateur Cup, which had brought them national fame two seasons earlier. The omission was probably due to a fixture list which had an overcrowded look about it before the season had even kicked off. The Portsmouth Senior Cup was also dropped by RA to the likely relief of the town's other sides after The Gunners' 44 goals in four games the previous season. To further ease the congestion, RA had to agree to play their Army Cup games in midweek as they sought to extend their remarkable record in the competition. Even then, victory in their first English Cup tie of the campaign would mean all Sgt Bonney's hard work having to be rearranged. Such was the club's tightly packed schedule. It was completed by the Hampshire Senior Cup.

The season began on September 4 in the worst possible manner for RA. They lost 5–1 at Eastleigh, ex-Gunners and all, in their Hampshire Senior League opener after going a goal up at half-time. The next game brought a 2–0 win at Southampton St Mary's Reserves with a more experienced side than the one with several fringe players who took on Eastleigh.

The lack of fit first-team regulars was picked up by the *Portsmouth Times*. It noted that more than half of the previous season's XI was missing. Phillips, Jardine and Coleman were the latest additions to the sick list.

Results barely improved. RA were fourth in the league with a record of: P4 W1 Dl L2 F4 A7 Pts 3 before they made their Southern League debut at the start of October. Bristol side Warmley were their opponents. The West Country outfit had finished tenth out of 13 second division clubs the season before. The position offered little comfort to The Gunners. A record of ten wins in 24 games had just left Warmley at the wrong end of a six-point gap which covered eight clubs.

RA were relishing the occasion in spite of any doubts about their early season form. Their team for the away fixture had been bolstered. Regular member Harms was joined at the back by Ward, of the East Lancashires, after he had impressed in the previous season's battles between the teams. Lewis was also drafted in.

The transfers, however, proved right the critics of RA's formation as an army superteam. *The Southern Daily Mail* called the practice poaching.

Lewis was tipped as RA's potential player of the season, wrongly as it turned out. The return of Jardine and Coleman also boosted the playing resources of The Gunners. Both were refreshed by a long holiday and Coleman had fully recovered from a leg injury.

However, the occasion fell flat. RA's poor form continued with a defeat by a goal in each half. The fact they did not disgrace themselves was a consolation and they proved quick learners by going on to suffer only one more loss in a 22-match campaign. Physically, though, RA took a battering at Warmley.

Several players spent the following week recovering. Forwards McCabe and Walsh were the worst injured. Walsh suffered a fierce kick in the leg and some heavy falls. The other first-team members including Jardine, rated by the *Portsmouth Evening News* as one of the best of the forwards, were reported to be training most days at the Men's Ground.

Their preparations for their next Southern League match, at Uxbridge, were briefly interrupted by the news they would be starting their latest defence of the Army Cup against the Royal Sussex Regiment at home. It was a game RA were to win 1–0. That was also the scoreline thanks to a second-half goal when they left Uxbridge on October 9 with their first Southern League win. Within days, The Gunners were bolstered by another new recruit, Woodard.

He had been capped eight times for the Suffolk County XI while his Yarmouth RA team had become the champions of Norfolk. But as The Gunners gained a new recruit, they lost an old favourite. It was reported Maxwell, a regular among their forwards in their first four games of the season and in 1895/96, would play no further part in the team's fortunes. He was to leave the army a short while later.

The Football edition of the Southern Daily MAil detailed RA's home debut in the Southern League.

News of another regular with the side's defence, Gnr Phillips, also appeared in the sports pages. Phillips, who had played in RA's Amateur Cup final in 1896 and was a two-time Army Cup winner returned to the Men's Ground as an interested spectator as RA's reserves recorded a 5–0 win in the United Services League against the 2nd Hants Volunteer Artillery. He had presumably left the army.

The Gunners' win at Uxbridge guaranteed a large crowd for RA's home debut in the Southern League a week later against Old St Stephen's in a game which was also the Londoners' first visit to Portsmouth.

They returned to Shepherd's Bush the victims of a 4–1 defeat and must have wished they hadn't bothered to turn up. A repeat of the 9–2 thrashing they received at the hands of Ryde earlier in the season seemed possible as RA went two goals up in the opening ten minutes to the delight of the 2,000 crowd.

Jardine scored both, the second from a well-judged corner from Coleman. A Walsh shot after a goalmouth scrum as Harm's free-kick hit the underside of the bar, together with a headed own goal by visiting full-back Woodward, completed the scoring for RA. The win moved them up to third place with an SL record of:

P3 W2 D0 L1 F5 A3 Pts 4.

But their opening day conquerors Warmley were clear at the top with a 100 per cent record from their first four games. Two cup draws were made before RA next tasted league action. The first pitted them away against the 2nd Battalion Scottish Rifles in the second round of the Army Cup. A day later, they were handed another away tie in the English Cup's third qualifying round. This time it was with their bitter Isle of Wight rivals of Cowes. The game attracted so much interest special boats were put on to ferry the spectators across the Solent. The island club spent the ten days between the draw and the match preparing for a big crowd, doubtless mindful of the explosive situation just a few months earlier. Any fears of a repeat were unfounded.

Some 2,000 people attended the October 30 cup clash. They saw a fast game in which both teams threatened before RA went ahead in the 80th minute through an unnamed scorer. The lead lasted just as long as it took Cowes to equalize from the re-start.

An unusually large crowd gathered at the US Men's Ground five days later to watch the replay end in another deadlock. The score on that occasion was 2–2 after extra time. Cowes had twice taken the lead, only to be pinned back by The Gunners. They secured the draw with a second-half shot by Coleman which gave visiting keeper Rylie no chance.

A fast and furious period of extra time failed to separate the teams and the tie went to a second replay. The venue was again Cowes' ground. It took the home side just eight minutes of all-out attacking to end RA's interest in the cup for another season in a game of intense excitement. But, as was often the case with the military team, another cup quickly offered them the chance to overcome their disappointment. Two days later, on November 10, they defeated Scottish Rifles 4–0 to take the next step to retaining the Army Cup. The victory was an easy one, despite the Rifles having previously knocked out Cowes from the Hampshire Senior Cup and fielding the same team which won the junior version of the cup the season before.

Cowes were also looming large again for RA. The teams clashed on November 13, for the fourth time in two weeks, and The Gunners emerged victorious at last to gain a single-goal Hampshire Senior League win. A third round Army Cup triumph by 3–1 over the 1st Battalion Worcestershire Regiment at Devonport ensured the winning ways continued.

All the cup action meant The Gunners had slipped to sixth in the Southern League, by the end of November with five points from just four games. Warmley continued to set the pace with a 100 per cent record from their seven matches in which they had conceded just two goals. RA took steps to improve their Southern League position when their first action in the league for five weeks ended in a decisive 2–0 home win over Dartford on November 27.

The game was one way traffic. RA's first goal summed up their dominance. It stemmed from a flowing move from defence. Hanna got the ball away from a corner, passed to Brazier, who sent it to Jardine. He made his way clear and sent in a centre which number eight Lewis was on the spot to convert smartly.

RA made it four unbeaten Southern League games in a row with a 4–1 victory against Royal Engineers Training Battalion (Chatham), the only other service side in the competition. Both teams agreed to forego half-time because of the bad light but it was clear the battalion lacked the combination and cleverness of their south coast rivals.

In spite of touching a free-kick into his own net, for the Kent side's goal, Reilly received a special mention for being applauded by the crowd for his clever work to ensure his side's dominance. After neatly clearing once, he patted the ball out to the halfway line in a repeat of his favourite crowd-pleasing tactic. Next for RA came a 3–2 away victory over a ten-man Southall before The Gunners treated 'the usual large crowd' at the Men's Ground to their record Southern League win on December 11.

Maidenhead were the victims by 9–0. They began, and ended, the game with just four points out of 14 compared to RA's pre-match total of 11 points. A five-goal first-half burst ensured The Gunners were sure to add to their haul, despite missing Coleman.

Brazier made light of the absence when he put RA in front from close range to end a constant bombardment of the Berkshire team's goal. He scored a second a few minutes later by helping the ball in from Hanna. Hanna netted the next with a 'clinking shot'. The procession of goals continued.

The fourth came from Meggs, courtesy of a Ward pass, and the right-winger added number five with a low shot. Haxton capped his Southern League debut when he made it six from one of a series of corners by Meggs. Brazier capped a fine game, with a hat-trick, by getting the seventh by rushing up and netting the ball after the beleaguered visiting keeper Johnson had saved from Hanna.

Kinman and Ward rounded off the scoring to add an emphatic touch to another win in the Southern League. The return fixture a week later saw Maidenhead suffer their second 5–0 home mauling by RA in three seasons. The Gunners made it nine consecutive league wins during a sensational match at Wycombe Wanderers, in Christmas week.

Yet again, controversy was present at RA's big occasion and, yet again, the spotlight of what little personal publicity surrounded late 19th Century football fell on Matt Reilly. His side were 3–1 up when the game at Wycombe's original ground of Adames Park exploded. A good-sized crowd had gathered for the match. Many of them ended up on the pitch.

The flashpoint came a few minutes from the end when Reilly clashed with a home forward. The keeper had saved a goalbound effort when Abbott charged him heavily. Reilly squared up to him and a blow was struck between the men. That signalled a pitch invasion and what the *Portsmouth Evening News* described as 'tumultuous scenes'. Order was eventually restored and play resumed. The closing minutes were scoreless.

The footballing aspect of the afternoon had seen Wycombe make the most of a strong wind at their backs during the opening period. But it took Butler 30 minutes to open the scoring. RA moved up a gear in the second half, doubtless helped by the wind. Patterson put them level with a long shot. He was followed on to the scoresheet by Brazier with a shot from a distinctly offside position. Kinman notched the third goal five minutes from time, just before the game erupted.

The two points kept RA in second place in the Southern League as 1897 ended. Their impressive record of eight wins and a draw from ten games put them three points adrift of Warmley with a game in hand and meant the opening day defeat by the Bristol club had been left far behind. But the Wycombe game's disturbance was to have repercussions for RA later in the season.

Its timing could not have been more ironic. A recent, unreported, disturbance at Eastney had drawn the local footballing authorities' attention to a lack of warning notices around grounds in the Portsmouth area. An FA rule stated: 'All clubs connected with the association must have printed and posted in their grounds, threatening with expulsion, any person who is guilty of insulting/improper behaviour towards the referee.'

Mockingly, in view of Reilly's behaviour, the only signs to be found around Portsmouth were displayed at the Men's Ground and the Officers' Ground. They made no difference as controversy and RA were again linked together in their next fixture. Reilly was at the centre of the matter once more. Just the identity of the opponents, already fierce local rivals Southampton, was different.

RA were a goal up in a benefit match for the Hampshire FA when Saints were awarded a penalty for pushing within the 12-yard line as they pressed strongly for an equalizer as the second-half opened. The Gunners disputed the decision and Reilly refused to move from one of his posts. He eventually agreed to stand in the centre of his goal to allow the kick to be taken and rushed out to meet MacMillan's shot. He was easily beaten.

A fluke goal allowed the Saints to go in front in the closing minutes. An attempted goalmouth clearance by home left-back Woodward, who had played a fine game, hit Meston and bounced into the net. RA had gone ahead before half-time through Meggs. His shot from Walsh's pass easily beat visiting goalkeeper Clawley.

The game lived up to its billing as a much-anticipated contest. The large crowd at the Men's Ground boosted Hampshire FA's funds by £40. As soon as Christmas was over, RA found themselves in another friendly. They proved too good by three goals to nil against a US League representative XI.

Undated, the picture is likely to have been taken at the end of the 1896/97 season. The trophies proudly on show are the Army Cup, on the plinth, with the Portsmouth Senior Cup in the foreground.

January 1898 – Record Times

The new year of 1898 began with bad news. Gnr Reilly was suspended for 14 days for striking a spectator during the infamous Wycombe match. The Buckinghamshire side were also punished for the incident. They were ordered to close their ground for a week in January and were forbidden to play within three miles of their ground. Reilly's sentence caused the *Portsmouth Times* to accuse the officials at the Southern League of double standards against military sides in a forerunner of the feelings of discrimination which were to become widespread a year later:

'Riots of this kind are very strictly punished now but had a lot of provocation, and the sentence seems rather severe for a first offence,' the newspaper's reporter commented.

'No doubt the league committee thought they were acting quite fairly, but it still seems to me that they are always rather hard when soldiers are the offenders, although why is a problem too difficult to solve.'

The year could only get better for RA – and it did. They shrugged off Reilly's absence to romp to their second biggest win of the season at home to another Bucks outfit. They hit eight past Chesham United. Reilly's stand-in, Paley, borrowed from the East Lancashire Regiment, let in just a consolation for the visitors in the dying minutes. RA's goals were shared between Jardine (2), Hanna (2), Meggs, Walsh and Brazier. An unidentified scorer from a Harms free-kick completed the rout.

The win was not enough to take RA to top spot in the Southern League's second division but revenge for their only defeat was around the corner. Before it could arrive, to take The Gunners to unprecedented heights, the league's honorary secretary showed how far the club had come.

Mr Nat Whittaker's comments, though, sounded a simultaneous death knell as Portsmouth's football enthusiasts were swept along in the tide of professionalism which was dominating the game in the south. Brighton, it was rumoured, were on the verge of becoming paid players and seeking admission to the league's first division. Such a feat was not beyond a Portsmouth outfit, according to Mr Whittaker.

In his opinion, the dockyard town with its population of 250,000 seemingly keen on football could support a 'really good team'. *The Portsmouth Evening News* greeted his comments warmly if warily. Such views had been expressed before but the difficulty on an island crammed with buildings had always been to secure a ground sufficiently near to the town centre:

'Whether Portsmouth will ever possess a "really good team" is hard to say, but local enthusiasts are to be found who say it's merely a question of time. They point to two or three factors which cannot be denied – a growth of interest in football among the youth of the town, among servicemen and among dockyardmen, many of whom come from the navy, and a steady increase of games and RA matches.

Any number between 2–4,000 now attend RA matches and exhibition games, and an experiment recently tried at Stamshaw showed close on 200 boys willing to pay for admission to a Portsmouth youth tournament. These are "signs of the times" which encourage those who look forward to some form of Portsmouth professional team. It's believed there are now several good players in the town who would gladly enjoy the chance of a "professional XI". They're now going to teams outside Portsmouth to play because there are opportunities for them as paid players in neighbouring towns and no scope for them in Portsmouth as amateurs. These, with some men from the navy, who would have to be men who would not demand too large a salary, would no doubt form the nucleus of a team which would in time move quite up to the standard of many clubs in towns of a similar size to Portsmouth.'

The article brought a rapid response from reader S.J.N. He wrote that a professional side in Portsmouth was certainly possible. The best way to raise a team would be to form a company with £1 shares. Many in the town would take up the offer, he suggested. The size of the footballing potential in Portsmouth was seen in a matter of days as arrangements were made by the authorities to cope with the crowds who watched RA when they played at the Officers' Ground.

A grandstand was to be built in the enclosure to rival the structures regularly packed at the Men's Ground across Burnaby Road. Until then, spectators at the Officers' Ground were exposed to the weather. The only accommodation was a pavilion restricted to officers and their friends. Special facilities had to be provided immediately at the Men's Ground to accommodate the large numbers anxious to see if The Gunners could reverse their only Southern League defeat. Extra entrances were created for the top-of-the-table clash with Warmley and, with the warm and sunny weather belying the late January date, soccer fans flocked to the game. At least 7,000 of them, RA's biggest crowd to date.

The interest was great enough to cause RA Reserves' game in the US League against RA (Hilsea) to be cancelled to allow the players to watch the first team. Professionals Warmley had held first place in the Southern League's second division since the season started. However, they had suffered one more defeat than RA. One loss was surprisingly at the hands of bottom club RETB and the other to West Herts the Saturday before the RA clash.

A third reverse was put on their playing record by the end of the afternoon in scenes never witnessed before in Portsmouth's footballing circles. The Gunners underwent special training during the week which led up to

United Services rugby club were the first major sports outfit to use the Burnaby Road venue.

the game to ensure they were in excellent condition at the kick-off. They played in their reserve colours of black and white.

They went into the match three points behind Warmley with two matches in hand. They finished it breathing down the Bristol side's necks in spite of their opponents' going a goal up through Greenwood, their number seven, during some fast and exciting play.

The home side drew level when a corner on Meggs's side bobbled about close to Matthews. He came out of his goal and Hanna sent the ball straight back with a header.

'There was a scene of wild excitement when it was seen The Gunners had equalized,'

the *Portsmouth Evening News* reporter wrote,

'and a thunder of applause went up such as was never heard at a football match ever played before on the Men's Ground. The mighty shout was very nearly equalled, however, a little later when RA attacked and Walsh beat Matthews with a hard shot in front of goal.'

The second-half saw RA's players in excellent style. They struck the crossbar from a Harms free-kick, though play was mostly confined to the home side's half. Reilly turned in a performance which won over the hearts of friends and foe alike. He was the object of specially enthusiastic attention when the final whistle went.

In an 'extraordinary demonstration', a large crowd assisted and cheered the Artillerymen into their barracks after their 2–1 victory. Referee Mr S.R. Carr also came in for praise, this time from the visitors. The official's firm enthusiasm and fairness to enable an exciting game to be carried through without any signs of ill-feeling was the cause of their thanks.

The gate money from the match amounted to £180 to confirm the attendance as being 7–8,000. But RA's success was already sowing the seeds of their own demise as Portsmouth's top footballing outfit.

Next to the victorious aftermath of the Warmley match, the *Portsmouth Evening News* reported the continuing support in the town for a professional club. "Wellwisher" was typical of the enthusiasts who had put pen to paper: 'There must be no half measures,' he wrote.

'Portsmouth will have to work on similar lines to those of the people of Bristol and get together from club teams from throughout the country the best possible men who are available so we might reasonably hope to see the team admitted to the Southern League and Western League in its first season. In the event of this, we should have attractive fixtures from the beginning but, equally, there must be no cheese-paring. On the other hand, if the consideration of the team is supposed to be a good one, support from the people of Portsmouth will undoubtedly rally to help those who are organizing the team and endeavour to make it one of the most successful teams (financial and otherwise) in the south of England.'

General agreement existed among the paper's readers the football club ought to be set up as

A modern view of Cambridge Barracks, which played host to many celebration dinners to mark the successes of RA.

a limited company with £1 shares. *The Portsmouth Times* added its voice of support based on the attendance at the Warmley game:

> '…*the gate at RA's match on Saturday conclusively proved that a really good team would be splendidly supported by the public.*'

An article in the *Hampshire Telegraph* asked anyone interested to contact Mr J.F. Wells, 38 Manners Road, Southsea. He was named as the secretary of the professional football club movement. He was also, apparently, connected with Southsea Rovers, one of RA's main local rivals.

Mr Wells was quoted in the *Southern Daily Mail* as saying the difficulties in setting up the professional outfit had been overcome. He thought its success was almost assured if the footballing public in Portsmouth gave their support.

Of much more parochial interest was the decision by the organizers of the United Services League, in which RA Reserves competed, to split it into two divisions. The reserves were seventh at the time with a moderate playing record of P11 W4 D3 L4 F19 A15 Pts 11.

Top were the Naval Depot with 11 wins and a draw from their 13 games.

Four RA players – Jerrard (goalkeeper), Turner (back), McKenzie (half-back) and McNeill (centre) – were selected for the league's fixture against Cowes. The island side won 2–0.

Meanwhile, the first team's increasingly dominant position on the local football scene brought about the further selection of four more players in the Hampshire FA team to take on Dorset at the US Recreation Ground, presumably the Men's Ground, on January 26. This followed the recent turnout of seven Gunners for the army in its 1–1 draw with Middlesex.

The contingent of keeper Reilly, Harms (back), half-back Hill and right-winger Hanna for the Dorset game was double the size of the next largest grouping, from Cowes. Just one Southampton player was picked. The game resulted in Harms and Hanna being awarded their county caps. Harms scored the second of the goals in Hampshire's two-goal victory.

A 40 game season was played by right-half Gunner Kinman as RA marched to promotion in the Southern League's second division of 1897/98. He was one of the most reliable players The Gunners could call upon that memorable season.

· C H A P T E R   F I F T E E N ·

January–April 1898
Champions

J anuary 1898 came to an end with RA on the road to their fellow Southern League newcomers St Alban's. The Gunners' drive for promotion was reinforced by two second-half goals from Hanna – with a good clever finish – and Jardine. But Reilly was the dominant presence again. He stopped 12 shots in keeping his fifth clean sheet in the league. He was only "beaten" by a disallowed goal by Long.

Another two-goal victory, at the Officer's Ground, over West Herts kept the winning run going. The game was said to have been of more than usual interest and attracted a large attendance. The visitors had been bolstered by several professionals since they had drawn 2–2 with RA in Hertfordshire three months earlier but the newcomers were swept aside as The Gunners gave a further demonstration of their growing confidence.

Next in RA's sights was retaining the Army Cup. A 4–1 lead inside the first 18 minutes against the 1st Royal Scots Fusiliers at Chatham in the fourth round paved the way to a 5–1 victory in front of a crowd of 1,500. The game was labelled as boring by the *Chatham and Rochester News* for being so one-sided. Its main preoccupation was the decision of the referee to reduce the home side to nine men. Half-back Craig and centre Lawne were ordered off by Captain Simpson after a rowdy scene:

'The inference was that they had insulted the referee but this was not so. Their offence was in using threatening language to Walsh, the RA centre. The punishment was altogether too severe for the offence. Much indignation was expressed over the decision of the referee.'

An equal crowd of fans, described as a 'fair number of spectators' gathered at the Men's Ground the same afternoon to watch RA Reserves defeat Rifle Depot 2–1 in the US League – such was the growing gulf off as well as on the pitch between RA and the rest of the service teams.

The gap was illustrated once more within a matter of days, again at Chatham. A Saturday visit by RA to take on the RETB in the Southern League ended in another 5–1 scoreline as The Gunners fought back from being a goal down at half-time. The win made it 11 league victories on the trot for RA and 14 games unbeaten in all, out of 15.

Back in Portsmouth, the reserve side, which had inched its way up to fifth in the US League, finished as runners-up in the senior section of the Portsmouth six-a-side tournament at Stamshaw Recreation Ground.

The reserves got off to a flying start in the annual event with a 4–0 win over Dockyard Athletic B. The Rifle Depot B team eventually proved too strong for The Gunners' second XI in the final by ten points (two goals, two corners) to five points (one goal, one corner). A total of 318 footballers, from 53 teams, took part in the competition to reflect the popularity of football.

RA had done so much to foster that interest and continued on their winning ways with another five-goal rout. Uxbridge were the latest victims and, so common was it to see fans flocking to watch the habitual home wins, the *Portsmouth Evening News* merely reported the presence at the Officers' Ground of the 'usual large crowd'. A hat-trick from Hanna and a goal each from Coleman, in his first game for two months, joined a successful Meggs long shot to allow RA to notch up another outstanding and promotion-enhancing performance. The success was almost matched by the reserves' 4–0 US League win against RA Depot.

The club's successes were being noted nationally. *The Morning Leader*'s edition of February 23 gave prominence to praising football in Portsmouth. Its reporter noted where the heart of the sport was:

> *There can be no doubt football is going ahead in leaps and bounds in Portsmouth since RA entered the Southern League second division. Gates have largely increased. Attendances are now never under 2,500. At the Warmley match, over £100 was netted. Until that fixture, the army champions had never experienced the pleasure of knowing their assets were over and above their liabilities.'*

The newspaper further commented on Reilly in its report on RA's rise. The publication urged the Irish selectors to consider The Gunners' stopper in their next international matches. The keeper failed to maintain a clean sheet in his side's next Southern League fixture, away to Dartford, but the single goal he conceded still allowed the unbeaten rally to be further stretched with a 2–1 win.

A five-point lead was now enjoyed by The Gunners at the top of the table over Warmley. *The Portsmouth Times* was convinced RA had sown up the title as March began with two months of the season still to go: 'The win at Dartford virtually ensures RA will be champions of the Southern League's second division.'

But championship form was sadly lacking in the following game, a Hampshire Senior League fixture, at Ryde on March 2. The Gunners' run of 17 successive wins in all competitions over four months ended as Reilly was beaten again. That successful strike by the islanders was enough to ensure his side only emerged with a point from a 1–1 draw. Both teams were reported to have played their best as the keen rivalry between the service side and Isle of Wight clubs continued.

Freemantle were the next opponents RA had to face in the Hampshire Senior League. The Southampton-based side had remained in the league despite their resignation from the Southern League the previous season. The fixture at the USMG attracted some 2,000 fans. They were kept waiting by the visitors' late arrival by 30 minutes. The delay seemed to disturb RA. They had to rely on a lucky goal from Meggs in the second-half for their win. The narrow victory coincided with the news RA faced a journey to Stoke to face the North Staffordshire Regiment in their latest Army Cup semi-final. The match against the Northern Ireland-based opponents was scheduled for March 24. RA's stuttering form, which could have been seen as a poor build-up to the important cup game, was swept aside following the cup draw with a dazzling 6–0 humbling of Wycombe Wanderers which contained no hint of a repeat of the trouble which marred the clubs' previous meeting.

By the interval, RA were four goals up, thanks to two goals from Hanna, one from McNeil and an own goal. The scoring spree continued with a further goal by Patterson and another by Hanna to give RA the wide margin of victory. The Buckinghamshire side used good combination and effective play on the ball to make up for the absence from the Southern League fixture of six regulars for a county fixture. They had an early chance which Reilly could only clear with difficulty.

But once Hanna had left Wycombe's keeper, Wheeler, helpless with a low shot into the corner of the net to put his side ahead the outcome was settled. The emphatic result took The Gunners' scoring rate to three and a half goals a league game. It also kept them at the top of the second division five points in front of Warmley with an unbeatable record of: P18 W16 Dl L1 F65 A13 Pts 33.

The scoring continued on March 12, three days later, as RA inflicted the first Hampshire Senior League defeat on leaders Eastleigh to exactly reverse the 5–1 opening day result between the teams. The convincing win was out of character for RA in that league. Their mixed fortunes had left them third out of seven clubs, with an unremarkable 12 points from nine games. Eastleigh, despite the drubbing at RA's hands, had 14 points from eight games, thanks to their previously unblemished record. In the 12-strong US League, RA Reserves were exactly mid-table.

A 3–1 win at Chesham in the Southern League and a further Hampshire Senior League victory, 2–1 against an Andover side propping up the table, completed RA's first team build-up to the Army Cup semi-final.

The growing interest in the service team prompted the go-ahead by the military authorities to enlarge the penny stand at the Men's Ground by 40ft on each side to provide better facilities so soon after the go-ahead was given for improvements to the Officers' Ground.

Football's growth in Victorian society generally was also shown by a planned extension to the Southern League's second division under discussion by Mr Whittaker. He was said to favour the formation of a south-western section to accommodate clubs such as RA, Cowes, Ryde and Eastleigh. A meeting at Easter was called to discuss the matter. But it was the Army Cup which occupied RA's minds as they set off on March 23 for Stoke for the semi-final that held one of the keys to their season. The Gunners triumphed at the penultimate stage again by overcoming the 2nd N Staffs Regiment.

The opponents failed to trouble Reilly directly throughout the 90 minutes as RA secured a 3–0 victory to keep their grip on the trophy for a further few weeks. The Gunners took advantage of the strong wind at their backs to go in two goals up at half-time, though the Staffords' had a strong defence.

Brazier headed in the opener from a corner. Hill added the second. RA's final goal, through an unnamed scorer, from a 'rush' came directly after the change of ends. The goal settled the match beyond doubt but the change in the weather from a storm into a blizzard meant the teams struggled in the final stages.

The weather was also dominant when RA returned to the business of winning Southern League promotion. Strong wind and rain made direct play impossible in their home fixture with St Albans. But RA proved the side better able to adapt to the poor conditions once again. The game ended in a 4–1 victory for them.

A repeat clean sheet was only denied by a Reilly slip as he went to save a soft shot from a Saints' forward. RA eased up in the final minutes, with the result secured, as the pace of their successful season came to a climax.

April's congested fixture list contained as many as eight games, topped by the Army Cup final against the Gordon Highlanders. Before that crowded prospect was a Southern League match facing Southall, The Middlesex side became RA's latest victims as they overcame the loss of stalwarts Hanna and Meggs to squeeze home 2–1. Completing the double enabled them to stay first in division two.

Hampshire Senior League 1897/98

	P	W	D	L	F	A	Pts
Eastleigh Athletic	12	10	0	2	51	13	20
Cowes	12	9	1	2	39	9	19
Royal Artillery (Portsmouth)	12	6	3	3	20	15	15
Southampton Res	12	6	0	6	11	20	12
Freemantle	12	4	1	7	18	24	9
Ryde	12	2	2	8	11	24	6
Andover	12	1	1	10	14	54	3
Bournemouth	record scrubbed						

April 1898 – Another Army Cup Final

A pril began badly, though. A Hampshire Senior League defeat away to a Southampton St Mary's Reserves side lower in the table was followed by a resounding 5–1 setback at the West London ground of Southern League rivals Old St Stephens. It was the first time RA had lost two fixtures back to back for six months. The Good Friday thumping in West London could be put down to the reserve side fielded by The Gunners to keep the first-team squad fit for the looming Army Cup final two days later. The finalists spent a few days at Guildford relaxing before the big match – a practice which was to prove fatal a year later. As final day dawned against the 2nd Gordon Highlanders, excursions left Portsmouth bound for Aldershot. The fare for the trains, scheduled to arrive at 12.17pm and 1.22pm, was 3s 6d.

RA went into the April 11 final boosted by a strong season, the *Portsmouth Evening News* reported. The difficulties in the opening games, caused by the absence of some of their regular players, had been overcome as they took on all-comers with success. In the Southern League, they had gradually worked their way to the top of the Second Division, dislodging the formidable professional outfit of Warmley in the process, as well as beating them in a record match of a record year.

Nine of The Gunners' first choice players had won the cup the previous year. Of the other two, Cook had joined Eastleigh and Coleman was out injured. Their places were taken by capable half-back Patterson and Brazier, a clever young forward from the reserves whose habit of worrying goalkeepers and backs had earned him the nickname of 'The Terrier'. The others were well-known for forming the best team in Portsmouth, according to the newspaper. Brief pen pictures printed in the build-up to the final showed how they had become individuals rather than just a collective whole.

Reilly: the best goalkeeper in the army; Harms and Phillips: two excellent backs, one noted for his good kicking, which was obviously of the greatest service, and the other for his steady, satisfactory work; Kinman and Hall: sound half-backs who did good and consistent, though unobtrusive, work; Hanna: popular captain, drawn to the thick of the fighting, did most of the work and captained his men thoroughly and willingly. Able to play anywhere in the team; Meggs, Walsh and Jardine: three forwards whose trickiness and dash had a helping hand in past seasons to carry RA to some notable wins. They had reached the final through the following victories:

R1 Royal Sussex Regiment (h) 1–0;

R2 2nd Battalion Scottish Rifles (h) 4–0

R3 1st Battalion Worcestershire Regiment (a) 3–1;

R4 1st Royal Scots (a) 5–1

S-f 2nd North Staffordshire Regiment (Stoke) 3–0

A total of 52 teams had entered the competition compared to the 64 when RA recorded their first success in 1895. The cup final opponents of The Gunners were stationed at Aldershot and led the town's league when the teams met. They were also Aldershot Senior and Junior Cup finalists and double winners of the Aldershot and Hampshire six-a-side tournaments. Added to the roll-call of honours was a final appearance in the Hampshire Senior Cup, in which they were defeated 2–0 by Eastleigh.

The destination for those supporters who made the journey to the final was Cranbrook Road Army Athletic Ground. Tickets, with admission from 6d to 2s, were selling quickly as the Easter weekend began. At least 500 servicemen signed up for the special trains. The expected crowd of between 10–15,000 proved to be an underestimate, with some 17,000 turning up on the day. But the RA supporters among them were left disappointed by the showing of the cup-holders.

The Gunners managed to hold out in the face of a strong wind until just before half-time. A good piece of individual work by Buist with some five minutes of the first-half left put the Highlanders ahead. RA's halves were mainly responsible for keeping their team in with a chance when a single mistake in front of goal would have meant a certain score for the Gordons. Kinman played a brilliant game and so did Hill. Patterson performed above his usual form. But the second-half was a different story. The Gunners went to pieces.

Harms and Phillips, especially the former, could not do their work. Hanna was virtually confined to kicking with his left leg, Jardine could only try hard, Meggs was very slow, and Walsh and Brazier could do nothing. On the other hand, the Gordons came out full of dash and spirit and played against the wind in excellent style.

Hall and Buist put in some good work and Watson tried Reilly with a shot which only a keeper of the first order could have stopped. The Gordons ran down and through RA again and again. They dominated the second period. The strike which sealed their win came when Hall headed home the ball following a mistake by Harms soon after half-time. The victors left the pitch apparently as fresh as they had entered it, with their pre-match training at Matlock the key to their fitness.

And so RA's bid to become the cupholders for the third time was over in their first defeat in the competition in two years and 13 ties. The Gordons deserved to win and their success was popular among the crowd. The result was greeted stoically by the *Portsmouth Evening News*:

'So the RA have lost possession of the Army Cup. It may be confessed that they played a disappointing game yesterday and that their opponents gave a fine exhibition of dashing football. The Gunners had a good deal of ill-luck in connection with the match. The semi-final, which was played at Stoke-on-Trent in a blizzard, upset the men for some time. And Hanna was so lame afterwards that he could hardly walk. Jardine was also lame and, in the final, he went wrong after five minutes of the start and was quite useless afterwards. Indeed, it would have been better if he had left the field at once instead of going on into the second-half. The Gordons were quick on the ball and gave RA hardly a chance. When RA did get opportunities, they did nothing with them. For instance, Meggs had the ball just on top of the bar from a corner when a low shot would most probably have scored.'

The Gordons' success was short-lived. Within a year, many of the players had been killed in South Africa in the build-up of tension which led to the Boer War.

April 1898 – Test Triumph

RA had to immediately overcome their disappointment at losing the cup. They had to lift themselves for a series of games which would determine if they would join the Southern League's elite to reward finishing as second division champions with just two defeats in 22 games. But before the test matches, the forerunners of today's play-offs, took place there was the matter of local pride against Cowes to be settled. The Hampshire Senior League game at the Men's Ground meant the most to the away side because they still had a say in the destination of the league shield.

The disturbances of the final fixture of the previous season were not repeated. The result was also different. The sides shared the points with a goal apiece. This meant Cowes had to settle for the runners-up spot in the table with 19 points from their 12 games compared to the 20 points gathered by Eastleigh. RA were a place further back with 15 points.

Three days later, on April 19, the Men's Ground played host to the struggling Midlands side of Wolverton London and North West Railway in the first of their four Southern League test matches.

Brazier scored the first-half goal which separated the sides. He made amends for missing an earlier close chance from a Hanna pass by shooting into the corner of the net past Waller's despairing drive. The keeper had previously suffered a bruising encounter with the home forwards as they battled for the lead.

A spell of pressure from The Gunners saw him fall as he got to the ball from a scrum in front of his goal. It looked as if the ball was over the goal-line but Waller threw it away. He again threw himself on it as Hanna made an attempt to net the rebound and it stayed outside the posts. All the RA forwards gathered around Waller as he laid on the ground. He received numerous kicks in the struggle and was forced to rest for a minute or two.

He recovered well enough to save from six successive home corners before RA took the lead. In the second-half, the early pressure was on his opposite number, Reilly. But RA again resumed the initiative before the visitors mounted a last desperate bid to equalize. Reilly was most severely tested from a free-kick awarded for hands. The midweek win against the First Division's bottom team, who had finished with just seven points from 22 games and conceded 82 goals, was followed by a 3–3 draw in the Midlands the following Saturday, April 23. Another major step towards the First Division was made in RA's next fixture the following week, They recorded a 3–1 win at Northfleet.

The game was Northfleet's last home match in the Southern League and it was one in which the *Northfleet and Swancombe Standard* acknowledged the superiority of The Gunners:

'The RA won their test match at Northfleet by playing The Cementers at their own game and beating them. It was a case of hard kicking and vigorous rushing and the soldiers were altogether too heavy for Northfleet in this style of play. All the same, the visitors did not play so superior a game as the 3–1 score indicates. In the first-half, they were two goals better than the 'Fleets'. But in the second-half, the latter team were decidedly the better lot and had hard luck in failing to draw level.'

It was too late for the home side by then. Kinman had given The Gunners the lead in the fifth minute. Brazier and Hanna added the further goals. But perhaps the most noticeable aspect of the game was the paltry attendance of 100. Such a visible lack of support led to a crisis meeting of Northfleet in early May at which it was unanimously agreed their dire financial state meant resigning from the Southern League to join the Kent League. The return leg between the sides at the Men's Ground on the last day of April was the biggest match local footballers had seen. In store for RA was the chance to play against the likes of Spurs and Southampton, both close to appearing in FA Cup finals, Bristol City, Reading and Swindon Town.

Northfleet had finished second-to-bottom among those clubs in the first division with a record of:

P22 W4 D3 L15 F29 A60 Pts 11.

They went into the crunch clash having already beaten RA's runners-up, Warmley, 3–1 in Kent and drawn with Wolverton. Those two teams were meeting on the same day but RA knew they had to make sure of clinching the promotion their table-topping form deserved with a win at the Men's Ground.

A sole second-half goal from Hanna assured them of that priceless victory. It was achieved in the face of relentless pressure from the visitors in spite of the fact they were missing three of their regular players. And RA had one player to thank for their success – Reilly. He was kept on the alert straight from the kick-off. He cleared twice, one of the feats being performed under difficult circumstances, it was reported.

RA relieved the threat for a time when Phillips worried Pittaway into conceding a corner from which Kinman headed behind. They pressed again and won another corner but it was only a temporary respite. The visitors returned to exert constant pressure. The second-half promised more of the same. Northfleet had the wind and sun behind them. Reilly again lifted the siege of the home goal. His clearance sent away Patterson, only for Lingham to rush out and claim the ball.

The attack signalled the start of a bout of pressure from The Gunners. Their front-line formed a cluster around the visiting keeper determined to score. Hanna succeeded as the minutes ticked away as he got behind the ball and sent it into the net with a cross-shot. One-nil to RA and the crowd's excitement was intense. Northfleet staged a fruitless late attack as the match ended. RA were promoted!!

Four years after the club's formation they were soon to take on the giants of the south. Warmley's emphatic 6–1 home win over Wolverton was only of academic interest. The one place on offer in the Southern League's top flight was heading for the centre of Portsmouth. The final look of RA's test match results confirmed the fact: P4 W3 D1 L0 F8 A4 Pts7

Southern League 1897/98 Second Division

	P	W	D	L	F	A	Pts
Royal Artillery (Portsmouth)	22	19	1	2	75	22	39
Warmley	22	19	0	3	108	15	38
West Herts	22	11	6	5	50	48	28
Uxbridge	22	11	2	9	39	57	24
St Albans	22	9	5	8	47	41	23
Dartford	22	11	0	11	68	55	22
Southall	22	8	2	12	49	61	18
Chesham	22	8	2	12	38	48	18
Old St Stephen's	22	7	2	13	47	66	16
Wycombe Wanderers	22	7	2	13	37	55	16
Maidenhead	22	4	4	14	27	81	12
Royal Engineers' Training Btn (Chatham)	22	4	2	16	26	62	10

Test Matches

Royal Artillery	1	0	Wolverton L and N W Railway
Northfleet	3	1	Warmley
Wolverton L and N W Railway	3	3	Royal Artillery
Northfleet	1	3	Royal Artillery
Wolverton L and N W Railway	1	1	Warmley
Royal Artillery	1	0	Northfleet
Warmley	6	1	Wolverton L and N W Railway
Warmley	D	D	Northfleet

> The committee of RA included:
> Col H.H. Crookenden, RA, (President)
> Major P.M. Brady
> Cpt H.C.C. Uniacke
> Lt H.W. Gardner

· C H A P T E R   E I G H T E E N ·

Summer 1898
Promotion and Problems

But a shadow was looming over RA even as the side enjoyed one of their greatest successes. That cloud could be summed up in one word: professionalism. As The Gunners took on Northfleet away, their victims in the 1897 Portsmouth Senior Cup final, Southsea Rovers, backed a successful application to join the Hampshire Senior League with a plan to turn professional.

The Rovers' idea was to form a company with a capital of £4–5,000 and apply to join the Southern League. The announcement was greeted with laughter by the delegates. Less of a laughing matter for RA, and more of a realistic idea, was the publication a few weeks later, in May, of a prospectus for the new Portsmouth professional club. The capital required was £8,000. The company was to be formed for the express purpose of buying and laying out four and a half acres of land in Goldsmith Avenue, *The Portsmouth Evening News* reported:

> *'It is the intention of the promoters to offer professional football as soon as possible and apply for the first division of the Southern League.'*

The hope of those behind the new outfit was that the club would become caught up in the general enthusiasm for football seen along the south coast and become the most popular form of winter recreation in Portsmouth. If the promoters wanted reassurance for their scheme, they had only to glance along the Solent to a Southampton side which had been Southern League champions for the past two seasons.

Three defeats in those 42 games confirmed the Saints' status as a top club in the region. Even RA's success in winning promotion, which could have cast a doubt upon the chances of the town of Portsmouth being allowed a second representative in the league's top-flight, did not seem to cause too many worries for the supporters of professionalism. They seemed willing to discount the fact only London, with Tottenham and Millwall, had two teams in the first division.

A *Portsmouth Evening News* journalist was just enthused by the thought of a professional outfit at a purpose-built ground. It would be a ground, moreover, which would be laid out with football and cricket pitches, and a cycling track, to ensure all-year round use:

> *'From a football point of view, the company should be assured of success if it is properly managed. The services of a good secretary and the engagement of 12 or so players of reputation should give the venture a good start.'*

Being denied entry to the Southern League's top division could be overcome, he added:

> *'…the point is a good team is bound to make its way. It can enter the English Cup and similar competitions and a couple of matches might be arranged versus the RA. When it has shown what it can do, the team might gain the coveted admission to the Southern League. If Southampton can*

form a team which is the pride of the south, surely Portsmouth can do the same? At all events, there is a very good chance of success for the company in excellent hands. It has a first class asset in the shape of a valuable ground, while football grows every season among more and more people in the borough and district.'

At least the reporter acknowledged the strength of RA as the dominant club in the town. But potentially bad news for The Gunners followed at the Southern League's annual meeting at the end of the month. It was agreed to increase the First Division from 12 to 18 clubs, while the Second Division was to more than double in size from 12 members to 26. All this could be seen as removing potential obstacles for the new Portsmouth club. RA were congratulated at the London meeting on their success in a formal acknowledgement of their elevation to Division One.

July was the next occasion RA were deemed to be newsworthy. The brief articles that concerned the club served to confirm how high their standing had risen in the ranks of southern soccer. Sgt Bonney was re-elected as the Portsmouth FA's vice-president at an annual meeting which celebrated one of the organization's most successful seasons.

The following week saw RSM Windrum chosen as one of the vice-presidents of the Hampshire FA. Another week further on and the RSM presided over the US League's annual meeting. He was unanimously chosen to again fill the role for the next year. It was confirmed RA's reserves would play in Division One of the expanded league in the 1898/99 season. They had ended the previous season fifth in the sole division in the only unremarkable aspect of RA's campaign.

Early August saw RA exempted from the English Cup's qualifying competition and the early rounds of the Army Cup as the preparations for the club's most exciting season got underway. Then came the news football fans in Portsmouth had spent four months anxiously waiting for – pre-season training would start at the Men's Ground on September 1. The date was earlier than usual but was, curiously, just two days before the club's Southern League first division opener.

The curtain raiser away to Swindon Town came three weeks before the next fixture against Reading, which would be RA's home debut of the season. Just as the training dawned, The Gunners place as the flag-bearers for football in Portsmouth was confirmed by the *Portsmouth Evening News*. There were plenty of familiar faces to carry the standard.

Local footballers, the newspaper said, would be keenly watching their exploits in the first division of the Southern League. The team would be pitted against a dozen of the best professional clubs in the region. The journalist continued:

'It's a good undertaking for an amateur team like the RA to be among so many professional XIs and the only one in the division. ...The Gunners did much better than anyone expected last season and it's not too much to hope this winter they will, at all events, keep off the bottom of the First Division. There will, of course, be some alterations in the team this winter, though all the old players will be available, except Kinman who has left the army and gone back home in the neighbourhood of Birmingham.'

Selection was automatic for one player. Reilly was set to take his place between the posts. Most of his team-mates were also fit and ready to fill their positions in the first team for the biggest footballing challenge of their lives. A 21-strong squad had been registered with the Southern League by RA. The newcomers were given a brief, and formal, introduction to the fans.

The chief addition to the squad was Clarke, Southsea Rovers' centre-forward and one of the Portsmouth area's best amateur players. He had obtained a commission in the RA and passed out as a lieutenant in Number Ten company, stationed at Clarence Barracks in the town. He would be available for the new campaign, though he was undergoing a course of instruction at Woolwich as his new colleagues prepared for training.

High hopes were held out by the *Portsmouth Evening News* for his prospects in stepping up several standards: 'He will no doubt improve by playing in the Southern League,' it commented.

Hanna, who had done so much sterling work for The Gunners as captain, introduced his younger brother to the club. Hanna junior was described as being small, young and born in Belfast. RA Reserves' outside-right McGibbon was also said to be a player likely to succeed when he was given a chance in the first team. Opportunities for other promising reserves were promised as well.

Only one friendly was lined up by RA before the season proper got underway. But there would be no shortage of fixtures once September arrived. RA had entered the English Cup, and the Amateur, Army and Portsmouth Senior Cups. Their exemptions from the qualifying rounds of two of the national competitions at least offset fear of fixture congestion, compared to the 47-game long season of 1897/98.

Sgt Hanna stayed as captain for the crucial season. Gnr Reilly remained as his vice-captain. RA's reserves faced the humbler fare of the Hampshire Junior Cup and the US League. Their captain was Gnr McNeil. Virtually the full first team turned out in the warm-up game against Hampshire Senior League side Rifle Depot. A large attendance for the game justified the *Portsmouth Evening News*' pre-season comments. RA's performance did not. They could only manage to squeeze home by a solitary goal from Brazier. Disappointment about that single second-half strike having to decide the game was coupled with anxiety as RA travelled to the County Ground, Swindon, to begin their campaign in the Southern League's first division on September 3.

CHAPTER NINETEEN

September – October 1898
Into the Top Flight

Reilly, Turner, Woodard, Lt Clarke, Phillips, Hanna, Coleman, Walsh, Phinn, Brazier and Jardine stepped out into history, and the unknown, in a kit of white shirts and blue shorts with a red stripe. A stunning goal from the halfway line by Phillips distinguished the debut in the higher echelon. But it was not enough.

New boy Clarke's availability was some compensation for the absences on leave of Hill and Patterson, who was in hospital having treatment for an abscess on his face. Clarke impressed with his speed and agility, and showed all the makings of being a brilliant half-back, in spite of being praised a few weeks earlier as a centre-forward. He and his new colleagues were up against opponents who included several former Football League players: backs Munro and Mills, once of Bristol Rovers, and half-backs Henderson (Preston NE), Logan (Sheffield Utd) and Smith (Third Lanark). All of them fine players and determined to improve on the Wiltshire club's previous showing of narrowly avoiding the relegation test matches.

With such opposition, and a lack of match practice for RA, pre-match guesses put The Gunners' result as anything from a 3–0 defeat to a 6–1 hiding. The actual outcome of a defeat by the odd goal in five could be seen as a victory of sorts. The visitors even stunned the 4,000 crowd by opening the scoring after 20 minutes. Brazier netted from a pass by Jardine.

RA's second, breathtaking goal built on the lead soon afterwards. A free-kick by Phillips from some 55 yards dipped into the net with home keeper Menham guilty of ball-watching. The success ended there. Swindon soon began to turn the game round, though it was not until the closing minutes that they got the winning goal from a free-kick.

Cambridge Barracks after 1853/54 and before it became the scene of many RA celebrations.

Consolations abounded for RA in the setback. The team worked splendidly together. Phillips and Hanna joined Clarke in forming a fine half-back trio and the forwards fought constantly for another goal. As for the back division, Turner did well while Reilly was Reilly, which was deemed to be sufficient praise. *The Portsmouth Evening News* could still see a promising season ahead:

> *'Everything considered then, RA did very well in losing by only one goal and only the knowledge of the severe trials yet to come prevents their supporters being enthusiastic about it. Four thousand spectators were thoroughly disabused of the idea that RA got into Division One luckily and not strictly on their merit. They gave their opponents' defence plenty to do at times and local critics were favourably impressed with their attack and defence. There's no doubt RA will be able to improve as they meet better teams. Several good points they presented will be brought out by the strengths and trials of the next few months.'*

The opening day fixture was followed by a blank Saturday, the first of two, and viewed as a welcome rest by an RA side yet to reach full fitness. A less charitable view was taken by the *Southern Daily Mail*:

> *'RA are without a game – rather a curious fact bearing in mind the necessity for immediate preparation for their arduous season's programme.'*

And, as was always seemingly the case with The Gunners, there was no shortage of bad news. Their exemption from the English Cup's qualifying rounds was suddenly withdrawn. They were faced instead with a first round home fixture against Weymouth.

More ominously for the long term was the staging of the statutory general meeting of the new Portsmouth FC, at the Sussex Hotel in Southsea. Those present were informed the company had bought its ground backed by £8,000 of capital. The directors declared their foresight by looking beyond the crop of potatoes which covered the land at the time. They could see a vision of a sports site turfed and fenced. Clearance work would begin after Christmas to allow time for the spuds to be sold off! The 4.5 acre site compared well to the three acres used for The Dell, the new home of the supposedly bigger Southampton club.

The Portsmouth directors' professional ambitions clearly set out, RA, football's amateur flagbearers in Portsmouth, were faced with the more mundane task of a friendly against the 'RA Remainder XI' in a much-needed attempt to boost their match fitness. The still parochial nature of the sport in the town was also shown by RA's fellow 20 members affiliated to the local football association for the new season. They included Portsmouth Grammar School, Hardway Rovers, Fareham Juniors and Gosport Progressives.

One well-known name was already missing from the list and its renewed absence must have caused RA's officers, already threatened with usurpation by the Portsmouth club, to seriously pause for thought once more. 15th Co RA were rumoured to have played their last game. Their loss was mourned in the press as being like that 'of an old and valued friend'. Since being formed in 1891, 15th Co had enjoyed a successful career for a team from an army company as James Tatton commented on in the *Football Mail* more than 50 years later.

They had been among the footballing pioneers in the Portsmouth district. At their peak, based at Fort Fareham, they were able to beat the likes of Southampton St Mary's. That memorable team – Field, Pitt, Moorhouse, Harper, Haxton, McManus, Jackson, Halling, Cooke, MacDonald, Nicholls – were the best players in the area at the time.

They got Depot RA (Gosport) into the Army Cup final in 1894, in a forerunner of the Portsmouth version of RA's first success. Several of the 15th Co winners were also with RA's successful team but the transfers didn't prevent their old team beating The Gunners by a single goal in the 1896 Portsmouth Cup Final.

The 15th Co team on that occasion still included the likes of Field, Moorhouse, Pitt, McManus, Haxton and Phinn. Goalkeeper Field, the back and team captain McManus and Phinn, the right-winger and occasional RA player, remained a couple of years later but the team's glory days had soon faded. They could only finish seventh in the previous season's US League after previous reports of their demise had proved to be premature.

A late entry for 1898/99 meant they were only allowed to be a member as a special case. All the fixtures had to be re-arranged to take account of the situation. But doubts continued as to whether they would make their first fixture, at home to 20th Co on October 10.

RA had no such worries. What they did have to concentrate on was building up their fitness and confidence to overcome a strong Ryde side – which could boast of the likes of former Burnley, Millwall and St Mirren player Christie in their ranks – in a friendly four days before they opened their home Southern League division one fixtures.

They failed and only heroics by that man Reilly kept the score down to a 1–0 defeat. His marvellous quickness stood between RA and the best part of six goals. The Island side did all the attacking, though it was not until less than ten minutes from time that Woodhouse scored the decisive goal.

He gave Reilly no chance. The Irishman made an impressive recovery to pull off two or three saves in as many minutes straight away. RA's front men, in contrast, were all at sea and lacked any combination. Hill's continued absence on furlough – or leave – from the half-back line was cited as one cause for the poor overall display. The influential player returned in time for his side's league opener against Reading on September 21. He helped RA to gain a creditable first point in a 1–1 draw against a side which had ended the previous season, their fifth in a league of which they were founders, in fifth position.

RA's next opponents could claim no such pedigree. Brighton United had been elected straight into the first division a few months earlier. In the sense of being newcomers, they and RA were equals. The Gunners' hopes of an easier match as they made their way along the south coast were soon in ruins. A demoralised side was overrun as RA crashed to their worst defeat of 8–0.

They were usually on the right side of scorelines of that magnitude, not suffering from them. Just as important as the result's effect on team morale was the message it sent out to the outfit's new rivals. RA's reputation was severely dented. The *Portsmouth Evening News* desperately tried to seek some solace amid the disappointment. It was not so easy a task as it had been following the Swindon defeat: *'The defeat will do some good if it leads to an overhaul of the team and a re-arrangement to strengthen the obvious weak spots,'* its reporter ventured. *'The verdict of RA supporters is that the return game next month will be a very different tale.'* But the simple truth which the journalist also recognised in his report was that The Gunners had quickly lost heart in the game. They were not helped by having to line up a man short for the game. Brighton took advantage of the situation by scoring two quick and easy goals. Reilly had the sun in his eyes and became blinded and totally forced out of the action. RA then gave up. Action in the second half was spent entirely around their goal which they defended in a half-hearted manner.

Their poor and spiritless display was summed up by the lack of concern the visiting forwards caused the Brighton defence. The promise of The Gunners' first two Southern League fixtures had evaporated in the space of less than 45 minutes. It looked more and more likely it was to be a long, hard winter ahead. The gloom was deepened by RA Reserves losing 2–3 against Rifle Depot in the Hampshire Telegraph Cup in spite of holding a 2–1 half-time lead.

To further worsen matters, RA's facilities came in for criticism. *The Portsmouth Evening News* lifted its eyes away from the first team's performances to lambast conditions at the Men's Ground as October got underway:

'The weekend rain will do an immense amount of good to grounds all round, but none have needed it so badly as the US Men's Ground. The state of the turf has, for a long time, been very bad indeed, not only on the principal pitch but on other portions of the ground. The curious thing about it is that cartloads of gravel seem to have been used to patch the ground with. The effect can be better imagined than described. This is the players' grievance. Spectators have one as well. Charges for ordinary midweek matches are too high. It can't be expected that football followers pay almost as much to see an unimportant Wednesday afternoon match as they could witness a first XI match for. The US ground people have done a lot to improve things for the thousands of spectators who now flock to see important matches, witness the excellent stand accommodation. They might follow up their enterprises by reducing ground charges. They could afford to do so.'

Next up on the gravelled pitch were Dorset side Weymouth in the first qualifying round of the English Cup. RA's team showed five changes from the one involved in the debacle at Brighton. The revamped side duly delivered a morale-boosting, five-goal victory.

The win brought RA the dubious honour of a home tie with Cowes. In the meantime, there was the matter of Millwall Athletic to deal with at the USMG. Runners-up in the Southern League two seasons earlier, the south east London club could boast a daunting playing staff of 16 professionals as well as two amateurs but had made a winless start to 1898/99.

They were too strong for RA. The Lions opened the scoring from a bout of goalmouth action after a free-kick but Reilly again proved The Gunners' man of the match. He foiled Millwall's hopes of a more convincing scoreline than the final one of 2–1 with one brilliant save after another. He was only beaten a second time by a penalty, while RA's scorer Meggs missed a spot-kick at the other end.

Players 1898–1899

Brazier
Bowyer
Clarke Lt
Coutts, J.
Coleman, H.C. Sgt
Dodds
Field , J.H.
Harms, H.R. Cpl
Harrison, E.
Hill, William Gnr
Hanna, John Sgt
Jardine, D. Gnr
Leach
McBirnie/MacBirnie
NcNeill/McNeil, Johnny Gnr
Meggs, James Bbr
McGibbon
Phinn, W.
Phillips, Davie Gnr
Patterson, William Gnr
Queenan
Reilly, Matt Gnr
Sutherland
Smith
Trainer
Turner, Harry Gnr
Taylor
Woodard, Frank
Woods
Walsh, Paddy Cpl
Willacks/Willocks
Whitehouse

October – November 1898
Tough Times

T he Gunners had little time to reflect on their latest setback. The games arrived thick and fast as October passed by in a whirl of fixtures. A 4–1 defeat on October 8 to a Southampton side on their way to a third successive league title saw ex-15th Co man Phinn score RA's lone reply for his second goal of the season. Regulars Walsh and Phillips were missing and RA obviously failed to match the Saints in their role as one of the Southern League's giants. The return from their opening five games showed this was becoming a common situation: P5 W0 D1 L4 F5 A18 Pt 1.

Those critics who questioned RA's elevation into the ranks of the professionals must have been feeling proud of themselves. The Gunners' reserves again added to the despondency around the Men's Ground. They were also without a win, from three games, in the US League. Their haul of a solitary point was just enough to keep them off the bottom of the ten-team division. RA Depot had that ignominy, with a 100 per cent record of the worst kind – seven defeats from seven games.

It's a fair bet RA's choice of their next opponents would have been anyone but Cowes. That, however, was the fixture in store in their next English Cup tie. The teams had a balanced outcome from their five meetings the previous season. They had won one game each and drawn the remaining three to continue the Island outfit's reputation as the only local side The Gunners had consistently failed to overcome amid their fierce rivalry.

Cowes were bolstered for the latest clash, in the cup's second qualifying round, by the inclusion of Dockerty as their captain. The half-back had previously turned out for Football League founders Derby County, and Luton Town, newcomers to the league's second division. His only previous clash with RA ended in a 6–1 victory for The Hatters in September 1895.

SOUTHAMPTON.

Robinson.

Nicol.   Meehan.

Meston.   Petrie.   Robertson.

Smith.   Stevens.   Hartley.   Wood.   McKenzie.

————O————

Gun. Jardine.   Corp. Meggs.
Gun. Brazier.   Corpl. Walsh.   Sergt. Coleman.

Sergt. Hanna.   Gun. Hill.   Gun. Patterson.

Gun. Phillips.   Gun. Turner.

Gun. Reilly.

PORTSMOUTH R.A.

Referee—MR. F. CRABTREE.

The matchcard for the of the October 8th fixture.
Courtesy of Chris Gibbs.

RA at least avoided the disgrace of a similar defeat in their next encounter. True to the sides' previous form, they fought out a 1–1 draw. But The Gunners' interest in the cup for the season ended across the Solent five days later. Reilly earned an ovation at half-time for a repeat of his brilliant form but the visitors were already heading out of the competition thanks to a two-goal burst in two minutes from Cowes. A further goal followed ten minutes before the final whistle.

The defeat took RA's season up to eight games overall. Just one had brought a win, two were drawn and five lost. The goals column made equally discomforting reading at F 11 and A 22. A first league win of the season on October 22 made a welcome improvement to the record.

Who better to achieve it against than Brighton United? A 2–0 win at the Officers' Ground over a side eighth in the table with two wins and three defeats from five games went a long way to repairing the severely dented pride felt in Portsmouth by the eight-goal humiliation a month earlier. Its impact on The Gunners' goal difference was less dramatic despite RA completely outplaying their professional opponents in the first-half when goals from Brazier and Hanna secured the win.

Proof that, for all their problems, RA were still far above any other local service club soon followed. It was the Army Cup, as usual, which allowed them the chance to play well. The first round draw put them against the 1st Battalion Rifle Brigade on the Isle of Wight for a tie which offered The Gunners the ideal chance to put their troubles on the pitch behind them.

The Rifle Brigade could boast of being the army's champions of Singapore two years earlier. But most of their best players had been moved on the return from the Far East. Added to which, RA knocked out the Brigade's predecessors, the 2nd Scottish Rifles, from the previous year's tournament.

'It must be safe,' the *Portsmouth Evening News* opined, 'that history will repeat itself this season.'

So it proved. A convincing 5–1 win at Newport left The Gunners easing their way through to the second round of a competition in which they had such a proud past. Hanna settled any nerves against the underdogs by quickly opening the scoring with a long shot. It was the prelude to a 4–0 half-time lead. RA were cruising.

They were rarely tested and, when the Rifles did manage to get forward, their shooting was erratic. RA must have wished all their opponents were so obliging. The 1st East Lancashire Regiment were next in line in the cup but October ended on another poor note for The Gunners. Just as RA's combined league and cup record started to look more respectable at: P10 W3 D2 L5 F18 A23 they suffered a 5–0 reverse. The latest tormentors were the fellow dockyard town of Chatham.

The North Kent side were one of the Southern League's most consistent performers and were plainly too good for the south coast team. Kind words for Reilly, despite the goals he conceded, were the main positive note in the *Chatham and Rochester News* about RA's performance:

> '...he fairly distinguished himself and frequently indulged in the practice of running a long
> way from goal, bouncing the ball in front of himself and clearing opponents every time. Turner
> and Phillips did well at back but the half-backs were only moderate and slow compared to the
> Chatham forwards. There was very little combination in the army front rank. This was the result
> of the effectiveness of the Chatham half-backs, who were in grand form.'

RA went on to face Warmley with their confidence again battered. The Bristol side had joined The Gunners in surmounting the challenges of the 1897/98 test matches in their first season in the South League. The Gunners had enjoyed generally good fortunes against the Western League's former top team. The run continued with a 2–2 draw as the Artillerymen again wore reserve colours – this time, maroon and pink.

For an even happier hunting ground, RA could turn again to the Army Cup and its second round. They repeated the feat of their previous tie, going in at half-time four goals up. This time, against the 1st East Lancs, the final result was even more emphatic.

They ran out 7–2 winners against their fellow Portsmouth outfit, with hat-tricks from Brazier and Hanna – the club's first of the season – ensuring an easy passage. The game's highlight for the delighted home fans came in the second-half with goal number six. The ball was passed from head to head among the RA forwards until it was eventually nodded into the net by Hanna for his second goal.

Hanna was the scorer again as RA battled their way to a precious Southern League point, their fifth, with a 1–1 draw at Gravesend United. Points were still equally hard to come by for the second XI. One win from five games found them in eighth place in the US League. The realities of the club's grim situation were brought clearly into view by the first team's next opponents.

A hat-trick from Gunner David Jardine played a large part in the only Portsmouth Senior Cup success enjoyed by RA. The outside-left achieved the feat of the only hat-trick scored by a gunner in a final when they played Southsea Rovers on March 20, 1897.

November–December 1898
More Praise for Reilly

Spurs had already established themselves in the Southern League as one of its more glamorous and famous outfits. The result of the clash with RA was 'a foregone conclusion', said the *Portsmouth Evening News*, though a rare pre-match article in the downbeat newspaper did hold out a glimmer of hope to the followers of The Gunners:

> '*Spurs are not doing as well as expected. They are fifth in the Southern League yet they are what is commonly called a "classy combination". But (it is) not generally known that RA beat Spurs on their own ground in October 1895.*'

RA had much the best of the game in that famous victory. Maxwell opened the scoring after eight minutes. Cook added a late second five minutes before the end to confirm RA's superiority after a second-half equalizer by the London team. Six survivors of the RA team remained four years on. Of that half-dozen, Reilly, Phillips, Patterson, Hanna and Jardine were in the team which stepped out to face Spurs on November 26.

Emergency arrangements were made to cope with the expected crush at the gates. The RA band added to the sense of occasion with a pre-match and half-time special medley of tunes. The Gunners created a sensation by turning out in black shirts.

But the redoubtable quintet were unable to reproduce their winning form. Matters looked promising when Walsh and McNeill scored, to give RA a 2–0 half-time lead, on a pitch saturated by rain, before Spurs rallied with a three-goal fightback to record a less then convincing win. The result did give RA some genuine cause for consolation.

Reilly, of course, gained special praise. *The Portsmouth Times* paid tribute to 'some splendid clearances':

> '*As a spectator yelled out when he pulled off his patting performance once: "You don't see that in London every day". Some of the Spurs simply looked on, lost I suppose in admiration.*'

Not enough, however, to make RA's league record any easier to read as December began. They still had just the solitary win over Brighton Utd to their credit with a form-book of: P10 W1 D3 L6 F12 A29 Pts 5. The figures had relegation written all over them.

But it was an off-the-pitch event unnoticed in the build-up to the Spurs game which was to have a more significant echo for RA later in the season. The incident happened in an otherwise

Maxwell, who scored an important goal in the Spurs game in 1895

unremarkable second round Hampshire Junior Cup tie. RA Res' defeat of Portsmouth Hornets was declared void because the Hornets' protested that the servicemen had fielded ineligible players. A replay was ordered before the winners could look forward to facing HMS Excellent in the next round.

Four months later, another team with a name which began with 'H' in another cup competition would lodge another protest with a more devastating impact on The Gunners. The reserves, though, put the row behind them to deliver a convincing 6–2 replay win. For the first team, that Saturday was spent travelling to face New Brompton. The journey back from North Kent must have seemed a long one. The game ended in a 2–1 defeat for The Gunners.

Consolation was increasingly harder to gain. Some solace could be found from RA's continued status as the Portsmouth area's best side whatever their results might suggest. The fact was confirmed in the Portsmouth FA team selected to take on Aldershot FA at the Officers' Ground. Six of the home team players involved in the 1–1 outcome were Gunners

Their squad, though, was about to suffer a major loss. Reliable midfield performer Meggs, a Portsmouth Senior Cup winner and Amateur Cup finalist, who had helped the team to gain promotion eight months earlier, left for good. He sailed for Ceylon (now Sri Lanka) in the first week of December. *The Portsmouth Evening News* was sorry to see him go.

> *'Meggs played for a good many years for RA and rendered good service in many hard-fought matches. Latterly, his performances were not so brilliant. But he will long be remembered for some fine exhibitions and the way he had in the old days of doing the right thing at critical moments of the game.'*

His former team-mate Reilly was also the subject of praise, on a national level. *Athletic News* carried the latest article to wax lyrical about the keeper:

> *'Gnr Reilly needs no introduction to the football world. Among the army's prolific yield of goalkeepers, Reilly stands head and shoulders over all. For RA in the Southern League, he is playing in magnificent form and has at least no equal in the whole of the south. The RA team has been comprised of two equal parts – Reilly and the rest. In Portsmouth, he is a public hero and how long he will continue to defy the best agents is a problem interesting to many. He commenced football as a Gaelic player in Ireland, seldom uses his feet and is too modest altogether for a man of his worth. He would reach the front of any team.'*

Reilly's next outing was in the Army Cup's third round at Devonport as RA showed how far advanced of the rest of army soccer they continued to be with another convincing win. The 1st Royal Welsh Fusiliers were humiliated 8–1 in front of 3,000 of their supporters. The glut of goals took RA's tally from the competition's three ties to 20.

The game's pattern was set as early as the first minute when Hanna put The Gunners ahead. The Fusiliers soon levelled through Davies but Hanna restored RA's lead a few minutes later with the first of two goals within a quarter of an hour to complete one of RA's quickest hat-tricks.

RA gave a fine exhibition of football as they built on their lead. Hill, McNeil and Brazier gave them a 6–1 interval lead. Play was more even in the second half. However, it was still one-sided enough to allow Jardine and Coleman to seal RA's victory without any further replies.

The game confirmed Hanna's status as The Gunners' leading scorer. The hat-trick, his second of the season and destined to become RA's last, gave him 11 goals. Brazier's six goals put him next in the *Portsmouth Evening News'* list. Five each from Jardine and Walsh put them in joint third place.

The reserves were at last adding some cheer of their own in the US League. A 4–2 win over 15th Co RA proved earlier tales of the latter's demise were exaggerated. But supporters of The Gunners could be forgiven if they had their attention focused elsewhere, on the pre-Christmas derby with Southampton. The overwhelming Army Cup success was the best build-up RA could have enjoyed. Local pride was also at stake with the 4–1 reverse along the coast two months earlier to avenge.

PLAN OF OLD PORTSMOUTH.

The length of St. Thomas's Street is a quarter of a mile.

REFERENCE.

1 Church of St. Thomas a Becket.
2 Garrison Church, old Domus Dei.
3 Old Mortar on Governor's Green.
4 "Royal George" Gun.
5 Old Fortifications remaining.
6 Old Fortifications remaining.
7 The Round Tower.
8 The Sally Port.
9 Old Semaphore Tower.
10 "Star & Garter" Hotel.
11 Old "Fountain" Hotel (now Soldiers Institute).
12 Old "Blue Posts" Inn.
13 The "George" Hotel.
14 The Museum.
15 Admiral Anson's House.
16 House where George Meredith was born.
17 House where the Duke of Buckingham was assassinated.

18 Admiral Lord Howe's House.
19 John Pound's House.
20 John Pound's Burial Place & Monument.
21 Chapel where John Wesley preached.
22 Old "Globe" Hotel—famous coaching ho.
23 Site of "Crown" Hotel.
24 Site of "Red Lion" Hotel.
25 Landport Gate.
26 The Quay Gate.
27 King James' Gate.
28 King William's Gate.
29 Admiral Palisser's House.
30 Kings Mill.
31 Mill Pond.
32 Mill Dam.
33 Where the Gibbet stood.
34 St. George's Church.
35 Site of "Three Tuns" Hotel
——— Line of Fortifications.

RA's grounds and barracks can clearly be seen in this map.

December 1898 – Derby Day

A record crowd of fully 8,000, according to one report, packed the Officer's Ground on December 17 to see if RA could restore their reputation. Walsh enabled them to go a long way towards that aim. RA overcame the absence of Hill from the half-back line because of an injured knee. Coutts took his place for his first appearance of 1898/99 in the first team against a visiting side which featured England goalkeeper Jack Robinson, a rival to Reilly's claim as the best stopper in the south, with fellow English international Harry Wood and Scottish cap Robertson, as his team-mates.

The tremendous number of spectators gave out a mighty roar in the first-half as Walsh levelled Keay's opener for the Saints. Neither goal was a clean cut affair. The first occurred when the ball slipped by Reilly as he tried to stop a straight shot from Keays.

Walsh's effort came as he just managed to tip the ball towards the visitors' goal before he and Robinson collided as the keeper rushed out to try to claim the loose ball. It hit a post and mustered enough momentum to roll into the net as the home fans held their breath.

RA held on for the draw, and the vital point it earned, as Saints pressed forward in the second half. It needed a goal-line clearance by Turner to ensure the visiting champions failed to complete a south coast double.

Christmas found The Gunners on the Isle of Wight for a friendly with Sandown Bay. Reilly played at left-back. His usual place between the posts was filled by Moss. The newcomer kept a clean sheet as the mixture of RA first teamers and reserves recorded a single-goal victory at the County Ground at Shanklin.

Reilly was back in his customary position on New Year's Eve for RA's Southern League win number two in game number 13. Their victory was, surprisingly, expected. Their victims were fellow amateurs Sheppey United. The visitors were reduced to that status through an inability to pay wages to their players.

They were finding life among the professionals every bit as hard as The Gunners and possessed an even worse playing record which anchored them to the foot of the first division. Hill was again missing for the fixture. He was joined on the sidelines by Brazier – seen in the stand smoking a cigar before the game – as a result of a left shoulder damaged in midweek training.

The second top goalscorer's place was taken by Queenan, fresh from the win on the island. The league debut-maker was described as a young reservist who learnt to play football in Scotland. He was faced with an Officers' Ground pitch in as bad a condition as the home side's playing record.

Before the kick-off, ground staff worked hard to fill out hollows – presumably with straw rather than the previously mentioned gravel – and spread straw around the Pavilion End. RA revelled in the mud. They had the better of the game and had the *Portsmouth Evening News*' journalist enthusing about their 'unusual commitment and cleverness on slippery ground'.

Hanna strengthened his place as RA's leading scorer by shooting the second-half winner. He had gathered his wits enough to put away a surprise chance shot after he was laid out just beforehand. Reilly performed his usual heroics and left-back Phillips made some valuable clearances to enable his side to resist Sheppey's late pressure to force a draw.

The game marked the halfway stage in RA's league season. *The Portsmouth Evening News* took the chance to assess the progress of a team which by its own reckoning interested and excited several thousand fans as they took on the south's leading sides. RA were not taking them on all that well but the newspaper claimed their supporters could still point to an 'improvement to a wonderful degree' as the season progressed:

> *'They possess a brilliant defence, plenty of pluck and dash and have covered themselves in glory in scores of encounters in which they have fought. They may not do so well this half of the season but the best wishes of all lovers of the game will be with them up to their last game in April.'*

The Gunners' occupied 11th position in the First Division, with eight points from 13 games. Below them were Brighton Utd, despite that convincing 8–0 win against RA, Warmley and Sheppey Utd. The Gunners were confident they could pull away from the foot of the table. It would undoubtedly have helped if all their games could have been at home.

A big difference existed between their playing records at the Officers' and Men's Grounds and on their travels. Every point they had gained had come from a home game with a record of: P8 W2 D4 L2.

A positive goal difference of 11–10 added to the impression of a side at ease on their own pitch. How different the story was away from Portsmouth.

All of their five games had ended in defeat. The goals column was a distinctly unhealthy F4–A22. RA had scored two of those goals in the opening day defeat at Swindon. One piece of consolation could be found in the nature of RA's total of seven losses. Four of them had been by a single goal.

The Army Cup provided a measure of the ability of RA to still compete with the best of the service teams around the country, with three wins out of three and 20 goals scored against just four conceded. The successes helped to boost the overall record of The Gunners to: P19 W6 D5 L8 F41 A40.

Hanna easily kept his top place in the *Portsmouth Evening News* list of goalscorers. His 12 goals was double the total of the next highest goal-getters – Brazier and Walsh.

January–February 1899
Cup Diversions

Events away from the pitch should have been of equal concern to RA and their supporters at the start of 1899. The team was completely disregarded by the Southern League's secretary, Mr Whittaker, as he took advantage of an interview by *The Sun* newspaper to back the new professional club in Portsmouth. He said:

> *'Personally, I think there's a great future for "soccer" generally in Portsmouth and if they can only do well next season the success of the club is assured. Help them? Of course I will, and anyone else who wants to make football grow in the south.'*

Mr Whittaker had long been enthusiastic about a professional team in the town and he went so far as to tell the newspaper he was confident the new side would be voted into the league by the other clubs at the annual meeting if they could point to a quality squad:

> *'You can take it from me that first-class professional football will penetrate all of the south and it is to that end the Southern League will direct its energies.'* he added with a missionary's zeal.

RA's forthcoming return fixture against Spurs seemed suddenly less significant. The year ahead, however, was to throw up challenges more far-reaching than even Mr Whittaker's backing for The Gunners' fledgling rivals across Portsea Island. It was a case of a new year and an old story as RA left Northumberland Park on the wrong end of another single-goal defeat. A crowd of 4,000 watched the latest loss.

A series of wasted chances by the home forwards helped the cause of The Gunners. Only McKay, in the second-half, managed to find the net in a keenly-contested game which saw RA have two 'goals' ruled out for offside. The second decision was the most controversial. *The Southern Daily Mail* thought Jardine had netted a perfectly legitimate effort. RA earned praise for a creditable display while, at the same time, fulfilling pre-match predictions they stood little chance of a win to extend their poor away form.

The newspaper's reporter, "Londoner", felt The Gunners equal in every department to their worthy opponents:

> *'In goal, Reilly was simply immense, while both Turner and Phillips defended splendidly, the first named being the finest back on the field. The halves also gave a sterling exhibition, Hanna especially shining, whilst Coleman, Jardine, Brazier and Walsh rendered a capital account of themselves among the forwards. The speed of the visitors quite upset their rivals' combination.'*

Two days later, and another fixture in the capital, ended in another setback and once more unsatisfactory. RA went down 6–0 to Millwall. North Kent proved an equally unhappy hunting ground again the following week as New Brompton's 2–0 win continued RA's failure to manage even a single away point.

The Gunners were at least better off than another North Kent side, Sheppey Utd, by one point from the same number of games and with a matching minus goal difference. Activities away from the pitch again cast a shadow over RA, with their meagre points total under threat. The single point they had gained from drawing with Warmley in early November was about to be deducted. The Bristol outfit were on the verge of withdrawing from the league.

A meeting of Warmley's shareholders was called and told the grim financial facts. The club was said to be £900 in debt. Only half of the amount was guaranteed. Gate takings averaged some £26 a week against £50 expenses. A legal meeting was under consideration to wind up the company which ran the club, they were told.

Warmley managed to stagger on. An outbreak of player power saw the team take over the running of the ailing club. Their first home fixture, after a 3–2 defeat at Brighton, was facing RA. Warmley's misfortune was RA's gain. The Gunners had their fair share of luck to thank for their first win, and points, on the road but it could be seen as some redress for all the single-goal defeats they had suffered.

The first slice of good fortune allowed Jardine to open the scoring before half-time after a period when his side's defence had been fully stretched. As they managed to break away at last, full-back McDermid missed badly and Jardine rushed in to score with a fine shot. Warmley were undaunted and continued to pour forward.

They were thwarted by Reilly and their own mistakes. Henderson, their centre-forward, once missed badly when he had the goal at his mercy. The home side did manage to score once but luck turned against them as RA were fortunate to regain the lead, through an unnamed scorer. And the continued weak shooting of the home forwards meant RA could enjoy the unusual experience of heading for home with two points to their credit.

The much-needed win was a good omen as RA prepared to renew their acquaintance with the Amateur Cup in its first round. They faced Kirkley, an Eastern Counties team with an Army Cup record equal to their own, and whose cup wins had brought them local fame. They had already won the Yarmouth Charity and Norfolk County cups in 1898/99 and boasted a record of just two defeats in 23 games. They failed in the task of tackling RA. The Gunners recorded a four-goal victory.

The Artillerymen had prepared with special training, which featured two cold showers a day (in mid-January!). But they would have done better to study Kirkley's involvement in the Amateur Cup before they started dreaming of a repeat of their feat of reaching the 1895/96 final. Kirkley had made their way to the semi-finals of the following year's competition only for protests from Marlow to lead to their expulsion for fielding a professional player.

Marlow, coincidentally, were the soldiers' next opponents in the cup's second round on February 11. Before then, RA built on that Southern League victory at Warmley by holding fifth-placed Chatham to a draw in front of 4,000 spectators at the Men's Ground. The visitors had gained their 15 points from 14 games. with the help of two Welsh internationals – ex-Manchester City full-back J. Harper and half-back Chapman. They could also boast of several other former Football League players' among their professionals.

None of them were likely to have experienced such a bizarre match as the return with RA in early February. The weather was so cold Hanna wore a sweater and the ball became misshapen midway through the second-half. Its erratic appearance caused many mistakes. None were needed to allow RA to equalize just seconds before half-time.

Patterson netted direct from a free-kick. His first goal that season ensured justice was done after Brazier had been the victim of a professional foul from Harper when he was through on goal. The visitors had gone in front soon after the kick-off thanks to left-winger Lawrence. Both sides continued to seek the winner as the game entered its second-half.

Reilly ensured RA stayed level with some masterly work. He was beaten once when a shot from Clements hit a stanchion and rebounded into play. The Gunners emerged with great credit from the game. They maintained their fine form with a 2–0 cup win at home to a Marlow club the proud possessors of a new stand for 250 spectators, courtesy of Saints.

A goal in each half from RA's Coleman and Coutts made sure the fans of the Buckinghamshire side would not be using their new facilities to cheer on their team in the Amateur Cup that season. Marlow went into the tie as underdogs. After all, they had taken three games in the previous round to dispose of Chesham Generals. 'Hardly in the same class as RA', sneered the *Portsmouth Evening News*.

Being regarded in that manner did Marlow, semi-finalists in the Berks and Bucks Cup, no harm. They fought all the way on a soaked pitch to frustrate The Gunners. RA's mood was not helped when a Walsh header from a free-kick by Turner was ruled out by referee Mr R.S. Worthing. The crowd's jeers turned to cheers as another free-kick by Turner was headed back across goal by Patterson for Coleman to score.

The floodgates refused to open for RA as Marlow fought back in the second-half. They were aided in their cause by the inability of Hanna to convert a twice-taken penalty after he had been sent sprawling in the mud following a run at the visiting defence.

His first spot-kick was saved by White. A re-take was ordered because several players had run forward before the ball was struck. Hanna wasted his second chance when he shot high over the bar. It took until a few minutes before the end before Coutts secured The Gunners' place in the next round. He opened his first team account from a quality cross from Jardine after a fine run.

More drama across the road at the Men's Ground that afternoon involved RA's reserves. They scored two goals as well in their US League fixture against RN Depot. But the 2–0 half-time lead they had established was wiped away as the sailors went on a seven-goal rampage. The spectacular collapse ironically began with a missed penalty by Depot's left-winger Compton.

The incident seemed to inspire his team as goal followed goal. The reserves were unable, or unwilling, to put up any resistance. The result left the second string with nine points from six games and halfway in a league reduced to eight clubs.

The match report of the win against Marlow was followed the next day by the information RA would have to travel to Harwich and Parkeston in the third round of the Amateur Cup two weeks later at the end of February. The Gunners were favourites to win the tie and go on to clinch the cup they had narrowly failed to win three years earlier.

February 1899 – Nemesis on the Coast

R A's success in being undefeated for four games was being increasingly played out against a background of the preparations for the new, professional, Portsmouth club. The latest news with regard to the infant outfit was the announcement of Frank Brettell as manager/secretary. His intended arrival in May from RA's recent double conquerors of Spurs seemed to match at least one of Mr Whittaker's prerequisites for a successful new club – that of an experienced manager.

Brettell's appointment was joined in the newspaper columns by a report of widespread rumours that Pompey's defence would consist of a quartet of players – Reilly, Turner, Hill and Hanna – lured from RA. The enthusiasts' gossip was strengthened by the addition to the board of Portsmouth's directors of The Gunners' treasurer and trainer, RSM Windrum.

The rumour mill also had Spurs players lined up as the forwards of the new outfit. One item of indisputable fact was the laying of Pompey's pitch as the death knell began to toll for RA. But The Gunners put all the speculation behind them in mid-February after the rain-enforced postponement of their Southern League fixture with Bedminster allowed them to focus their attentions on their forthcoming Amateur Cup quarter-final tie with Harwich and Parkeston.

The regular first team of: Reilly, Turner, Phillips, Coutts, Hill, Patterson, Coleman, Walsh, Hanna, Brazier and Jardine, plus reserves Woodard and McNeil, were taken by the club to spend a week in the Suffolk coastal town of Aldeburgh for some quiet preparation for the big game. They had practised a similar routine before. But a further part of the death knell was sounding for their future. Sgt Bonney, in a pre-match message from RA's base at The White Lion Hotel, told the *Portsmouth Evening News* his team were 'in excellent mettle' for the crucial tie. The only irritation had been the army's 4–3 defeat by Middlesex at the Officers' Ground. The result annoyed the players, he said, because they would have liked to have played. *The Portsmouth Times* was confident, in its match day edition of February 25, RA had made the right decision in staying at Aldeburgh:

> *They will thus turn out fresh and not fatigued with a long train journey, as if they had gone up yesterday. And, good though the Essex men might play, the result should not be in doubt… and the possibilities of the cup coming to Pompey are bright.'*

Those sentiments were shared by *Southern Daily Mail*:

> *'After their long rest and training on the Suffolk coast, the RA ought to be able to render a good account of themselves.'*

The team moved on to spend the eve of the match in quarters specially prepared for them at Harwich's Redoubt. Match day found the *Harwich and Dovercourt Newsman* informing its readers about RA's training:

> *'As almost everyone has heard, the RA have gone to Aldeburgh to get themselves in the best of conditions for their bout with The Shrimpers. Now a week's thorough training to a team like Portsmouth means that Harwich have a stupendous task before them. But, as the latter have*

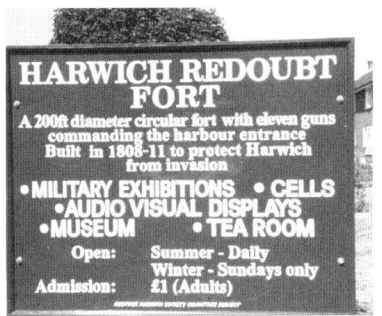

Harwich Redoubt still presents a solid site along the Essex Coast.

been a bit enthusiastic too in their training and exercise this week, they are almost bound to provide a handful for the Artillerymen…'

RA lived up to their billing and Sgt Bonney's description of their condition when they took on the home side top of the seven-team North Essex League with a 100% record from six games and 28 goals scored compared to just two against.

The Gunners more than doubled that goals against tally as they entered the semi-final draw thanks to a fine 3–1 win against their hosts in front of a record crowd officially numbered at 4–5,000 and unofficially at nearer 11,000 when those on a free vantage point known locally as Jew's Hill were included.

Within hours, it was apparent they had seen the most hollow of victories by the military side. *The Walton Gazette* set the scene for RA's downfall at the Royal Oak Ground in Harwich's Dovercourt district:

'The turf was in excellent condition, and the weather was delightfully fine, there being a fresh easterly wind blowing down the ground.'

In a bizarre twist, Southern League secretary Nat Whittaker, among the firmest supporters of a professional Portsmouth side, was one of the linesmen. An early goal by Hanna sent The Gunners on their way in the tie.

The captain put them in the lead with a beautiful cross-shot in the sixth minute as they started at a pace which quickly forced the home side to retreat. The bad start worsened for Harwich when Reilly saved a penalty from full-back Bacon to keep RA in front at half-time. It was the only shot the keeper had to save all game.

Brazier added a second goal for The Gunners after a spell of Harwich pressure as the second-half opened. Coleman began the vital move as he ran with the ball before a pass sent away Walsh. The forward ran almost to the goal-line before he pulled back the ball for Brazier to hit it home.

The Harwich supporters finally had something to cheer about as The Shrimpers netted, though the scorer's identity was confused in the local newspapers. One named him as right-winger Taylor. The other attributed the accolade to Eley, the number eight, who took advantage of confusion between Phillips and Reilly.

But it was an academic effort. Hanna netted his second goal of the game, and RA's third, to restore the visitors' two-goal lead and make up for an earlier miss, from the penalty spot after Howard had handled. The result allowed the Amateur Cup favourites to complete another step towards their predicted place in the final:

'The easterners, it was true, had a big reputation in their own part of the world and were foes to be respected on their own turf,' the Portsmouth Times *ventured in its match report on March 4. 'But it takes more than the average civilian amateur XI to lower The Gunners' colours. All through the game, the visitors played like a winning team, their combination being immensely superior to that of their opponents while Turner and Phillips were much too good for the home rearguard. The final score was 3–1 but, with a different goalkeeper than Kettle, Harwich would probably have received a much worse licking, he giving a really brilliant display … if the cup doesn't come to Portsmouth it will be almost a modern miracle.'*

Harwich and Parkeston's executive committee thought otherwise when its members met immediately after the game. They lodged a protest with the cup committee of the cup on the grounds that The Gunners were not a bona fide amateur club as defined by the competition's rules.

February 1899
'Professionalism' Protests

The first indication that RA's victory could fail to be another stepping stone towards winning the Amateur Cup arrived in the following Monday's edition of the *Southern Daily Mail*. The newspaper told its readers that The Gunners' stay at Aldeburgh had angered the East Coast residents for being against the ethics of amateurism:

'Perhaps it would be interesting to mention that RA's short holiday at Aldeburgh caused widespread indignation in East Anglia. And the local journals were freely condemning the military authorities at Portsmouth for granting the men the week's furlough! However, "where ignorance is bliss" and co, and The Gunners can afford to treat such jealous expressions of opinion with the contempt they deserve. What is the difference between the Corinthians and the Casuals – not to mention dozens of minor clubs – who have their tours at Christmas and Easter and the RA's spending a week's holiday? In every case, the expenses are met by gate money.'

It was March 2 before the FA officially confirmed the nature of Harwich's protest Mr F.J. Wall, the FA's long-serving secretary, contacted Sgt Bonney with the news. He began the Artillerymen's desperate battle with football's hierarchy for their survival. The Gunners were still paired with Grimsby All Saints in a semi-final to be played in London on March 3 but Harwich and Parkeston's name also went into the hat.

The dispute, as the *Southern Daily Mail* had reported, centred around Harwich and Parkeston's claim that RA's players had acted as professionals by enjoying the all-expenses paid break at Aldeburgh, which included an outing to the Crystal Palace in South London. The action had broken the FA's strict rules on amateurism, it was alleged. Rule 26 stated:

'Any player registering with the FA as a professional, or of receiving remuneration, or of consideration of any sort, after necessary travelling and total expenses actually paid, should be considered to be a professional.'

The Essex club's local press viewed the issue as a defining moment, no less, in the ongoing fight between those who played the game for love and those who played for money.

The newspapers' initial admiration for their club's ability to put on a good display against the stronger RA team soon turned to complaints at the way the south coast team had prepared for the game. As March 1899 went on, so their criticism continued. *The Harwich and Dovercourt Free Press*' reporter "Critic" disagreed with the views in RA's favour expressed in the national *Morning News* when he said:

'Military teams have more advantages than civilian but the RA in addition took a week's private training, drawing on the club to defray the expenses of the same, thus clearly violating two of the rules of amateurism.'

The result of RA's protest, the newspaper continued:

> 'is being watched by a large number of clubs as the case, being a test one, will define the difference between an amateur and a professional.'

For the *Harwich and Dovercourt Newsman*, no doubt existed about RA's guilt in a matter which had played a large part in their victory against the home side:

> 'As everybody probably knows… the RA have been struck out of the competition on the ground of infringement of the amateur rules, which do not permit amateur teams to spend a week's holiday at the seaside, with wines, cigars and billiards thrown in as well as their hotel and travelling expenses.'

Folklore has included wines £2 9s, billiards £2 4s, cigars £1 11s 3d and carriages at £6 6s among the expenses incurred by RA at The White Lion Hotel. The hotel, which still survives, has been unable to confirm if these items helped to make up RA's tariff.

But the total bill was reported in the *Southern Daily Mail* as being £64. That would appear to offer plenty of scope for high living at a time when it cost £25 a year to rent a small house in Portsmouth, £250 could buy a seven-roomed house in North End and a cook was paid an annual salary of £20 and housemaid £14.

Whatever the truth of RA's stay, the FA Amateur Cup committee – which had the power to expel The Gunners if they were declared professionals – fixed its meeting to consider the protests for March 6. RA's future hung in the balance.

March 1899
Honour for Hanna

The season had to continue, however. The Army FA was trying to secure the Aston Lower Grounds, also known as Villa Park, in Birmingham for The Gunners' Army Cup semi-final against the 1st Battalion South Lancashire Regiment from Preston. The Southern League fixtures also demanded attention. RA's first league game in a month took them to Gravesend just before the cup emergency committee was due to hold its deliberations. The game coincided with a first international cap awarded to a Gunner, and to any footballer in Portsmouth, in another instance of the contrasting fortunes which afflicted the history of the club.

Their popular captain Hanna, was chosen for the Ireland team to play Wales at the Distillery ground in Belfast on March 4. He received mixed reviews for his part in his country's 1–0 win. *The Portsmouth Times* commented:

> *'The newspaper critics appear to considerably differ as to Hanna's playing at centre-forward for Ireland on Saturday, some praising him and others doing vice-versa. But a man can hardly be expected to show his best form when playing with utter strangers and many authorities think the XI should be selected en bloc to meet Scotland. Why, however, Reilly has not got his cap is a mystery which only the Irish selection committee can explain.'*

The keeper backed the comments with his display in RA's Southern League game at Gravesend. But the game ended badly for The Gunners. They had not tasted defeat for six weeks. The renewed experience was none the better for that, though. The home side were the better throughout and attacked constantly. They achieved their 3–0 win in spite of meeting Reilly in fine form, seeing other shots miss the goal by a few inches and having one hit the bar.

The result augured badly for the bigger battle RA faced at the committee meeting. That also ended in defeat. The club's future looked bleak after the cup committee's members – under the presidency of G.S. Sherrington, of Ipswich, one of the FA's vice-presidents – upheld Harwich and Parkeston's protests after more than two hours of consideration at Chancery Lane in central London. The committee resolved:

> *'From the facts brought before it, the Amateur Cup committee finds the RA (P) have broken Rule 26 of the FA and, therefore, that the protest be sustained and that RA be removed from the Amateur Cup competition and the match awarded to Harwich and Parkeston.'*

The carpings of *Truth* magazine four years earlier about RA's status had been revisited with a vengeance. Indignation was the reaction of the *Portsmouth Times* to the findings compared to its indifference when the protest was revealed. Its initial view: 'It's hard to see on what grounds Harwich base their protests against the RA' had turned to scorn in its March 11 edition:

'The decision of the emergency committee on the protest of Harwich against RA came as a great surprise for it's hard to see how undergoing a week's special training at Aldeburgh can be a breach of the amateur rules, considering the expenses were paid out of the gate money by the club. The Harwich men held that the special training was not absolutely necessary to the playing of the tie. And that it gave an undue advantage to the clubs able and willing to give their players a course of training over those who were unable to do so. What wonderful logic! According to this view, clubs that get big gates should not be allowed to enter for the cup. But it might be argued that, if proper clubs can't properly afford to train their men, they should not enter at all. However, the committee decided that there had been a technical infringement of the rule, though this does not apply to the Army Cup. So, for the third time The Gunners have had to relinquish all hopes of capturing the trophy, which is all the more disappointing from the fact that they were universally looked upon as the likely winners.'

A week later, and the newspaper's mood had turned even uglier. It called the FA Amateur Cup emergency committee biased:

'In fact, it's impossible to see what grounds the committee had for a decision which was evidently dictated by jealousy and antagonism to military football when they prove too strong for their (so called) amateur civilian rivals.'

Athletic News, often among the admirers of RA, also took up the club's stance as March wore on:

'The disqualification of the RA(P) from the Amateur Cup has given great offence in the naval town where the real facts about military football are well known. At present, the club occupies the anomalous position of being disqualified for professionalism and yet not being declared such, or asked to disprove the charge. The rule in question says that any amateur player receiving remuneration/consideration above his necessary travelling and hotel expenses actually paid shall be a professional. There are two points to consider. First, the word "necessary". If the club thought it necessary to give the men the training, and the hotel expenses were only the necessary ones, how is a player to be made a professional? Again, is not the rule intended rather to stop a player benefiting in pocket by his playing and that alone? If it's otherwise, the Corinthians who

Wines, cigars and billiards made up part of PA's training at the White Lion Hotel at Aldeburgh, in Suffolk, as they prepared for their Amateur Cup quarter-final against Harwich and Parkeston in 1898/99.

had that South African free trip recently, should be called upon to explain. It's a very serious thing to interfere with the common-sense practice of amateurism. For instance, if a week's training is breaking the rules, so is five minutes or if a £40 hotel bill is an infringement, so is a glass of beer and a sandwich. The bona fides of the RA are so well known that, even if their action is held to have broken the rule, it was a pure misadventure and, if the team are thus thrown out of the Amateur Cup, it will be extraordinary. If an appeal finds them not guilty, who will re-instate them in the Amateur Cup?'*

The *Southern Daily Mail* adopted a more relaxed tone on the issue and said hope still remained for The Gunners:

'This ruling, on the face of it, places the soldiers on the same footing as a professional club but that their bona fides in the matter were taken into consideration was evident by the rider added to the ruling to the effect that it only applied to the Amateur Cup, and not to the Army Cup. Though protesting against the soldiers, the Harwich club officials spoke in eulogistic terms of the straightforward manner in which RA had acted in the case. Everything that the Harwich club has put forward was frankly admitted and the RA simply put in the plea that, if the rule had been broken, it was broken in ignorance. Sympathy will certainly go with the soldiers for the cup was well within their grasp. But now they will have to wait for at least another year before they have another chance of securing the cup.'

But the newspaper did say caustically of RA's opponents in that fateful match:

'The RA are not given to protesting when they are beaten but it's a curious fact that reinstated professionals and old soldiers who have settled at Harwich are the backbone of the East Anglian team.'

It was revealed with a sense of awry timing alongside the committee's findings RA had received £30, more than enough to cover their appeal costs, as their share of the gate receipts from that ill-fated encounter on the Essex coast.

One bright spot for The Gunners on a day when their future seemed bleak concerned their rivals for the Southern League's wooden spoon, Sheppey. The Kent side had lost one of its best players, Arthur Rule, to Spurs. Centre-half Herbert Abbott was also about to depart on Admiralty orders to Malta dockyard.

But it was the 46 words from the emergency committee which dominated the sporting news in Portsmouth. They ruined in one sentence five years work by RA in becoming the town's footballing flagship. They were effectively finished.

Y. FEBRUARY 27 1899

FOOTBALL.

AMATEUR CUP.

Draw for the Semi-Final—Probable Protest Against the R.A.

The Amateur Cup Committee met this afternoon, and made the draw for the semi-final of the competition, which resulted as follows :—
Stockton v. Old Malvernians, at Darlington.
R.A. or Harwich and Parkeston v Grimsby, All Saints, in London.
To be played March 11th.
From the above it would appear that Harwich have entered a protest on some ground or another in reference to Saturday's match—probably on account of the R.A. having spent a week in training at Aldeburgh, a circumstance which some consider as opposed to the ethics of amateurism.

NOTES ON SATURDAY'S GAME.
(By Our Own Reporter.)

Before dealing with Saturday's match, perhaps it would be interesting to mention that the R.A.'s short holiday at Aldeburgh caused widespread indignation in East Anglia, and the local journals

How the Southern Daily Mail reported the first news of the protest by Harwich and Parkeston.

March 1899
A Challenging Period

Undaunted, RA's officials immediately challenged the committee's verdict which sent them out of the Amateur Cup without losing a game. A brief conference among the officials ended with the decision to pay a £25 appeal fee. The members of the committee had also wasted no time. They had already decided the venue for Harwich and Parkeston's semi-final tussle with Grimsby All Saints the following Saturday. A lack of suitable grounds forced a change from the original choice of London to the Portman Road ground at Ipswich, a few miles from Harwich. Semi-final day of March 11 dawned with RA shrouded in gloom instead of being bathed in glory.

As Harwich and Parkeston kicked off, on their way to a win through a two-goal fightback in the second-half, RA began their home Southern League match with Swindon as a side in limbo.

Their supporters, players and officials had a few hours earlier experienced the final nail in the club's coffin being publicly hammered in. The appeal against the cup expulsion had been dismissed by the emergency committee. Its damning verdict stated:

'That the payment by the club of the training expenses of the players at Aldeburgh, and of the expenses of the visit of the players to Crystal Palace, in both respects constitute infringement of their status as amateurs. They must be deemed to be professionals under the rules and must be registered as such.'

The announcement was greeted almost with indifference by the *Southern Daily Mail*:

'After the decision by the Amateur Cup committee, it was only to be expected The Gunners would be declared professionals. So, this morning's announcement will not occasion any great disappointment. But some surprise must be felt that the Crystal Palace trip has been questioned. This opens up still further possibilities, and it now remains to be seen what action the Army FA will take.'

Sgt Bonney had heard the committee's verdict privately the previous evening. He told the newspaper he had immediately spent another £25 on a further appeal. The appeal had to be heard within 18 days. As well as presenting a possible lifeline, the move allowed The Gunners to continue their Southern League fixtures.

But there was no doubt RA were facing their abolition on March 11 as they stepped out against the visitors from Wiltshire for their first league match at the Men's Ground for five weeks. The furore about the club's status brought a large crowd to line the ropes. Hanna, the team captain, was the first of the "professionals", as the press described them, to run out on to the pitch.

Just a week before he had reached the heights of the game when he helped Ireland to a 1–0 win against Wales in Belfast. A week, though, had turned out to be a very long time. He was left in no doubt of the spectators' affections, being warmly greeted as he appeared on the pitch. The effect of the rousing reception was joined by a welcome victory to lift some of the despondency from the club's collective shoulders. But nothing could make up for the fact they should have been contesting the Amateur Cup semi-final. RA's players seemed determined to make up for the dilemma in which they were caught. They scored the winner in the first-half.

Jardine got a good pass from Brazier to send in a low centre. Menham, the visitors' keeper, fell as he met the ball and Hanna nudged it into the net. RA were helped by an injury to Swindon's centre-half, Smith, and they finished the stronger side to reverse their opening day defeat, though their aggressive tactics were criticised in the press.

That early win had set up Swindon for a fine season. Up to the loss against RA, they had gained 18 points from 18 games. RA, by comparison, had just 11 points with an extra game played.

March 1899 – Cup Misery

RA's victory had marked the end of a parochial chapter in the club's history on top of the emergency committee's judgement, which threatened a total severing with the past. It was the first league match to be staged at the Men's Ground since the retirement of Mr W. Richards after 22 years as the sporting venue's caretaker. He ended his long association, in which he had seen RA develop and grow, in mid-February. *The Hampshire Telegraph* paid tribute to his work. Previous criticisms of the condition of the pitch were cast aside:

> *'Mr Richards has seen a wide development of sport – especially football – and many enthusiastic habitués of the ground will regret his departure. During his contact with the ground, Mr Richards has been most assiduous and energetic in the discharge of his duties. And the splendid condition of the turf has oft-times been the subject of warm praise and congratulation. Mr Richards was formerly a colour sergeant in the RMLI and, upon retirement from that corps on pension, he was appointed to his present position.'*

RA's next game, five days later, was far away from the familiar and comforting surroundings of the Men's Ground, They made their way to the Lower Aston Grounds to contest the Army Cup semi-final. Their progress in the competition had been overshadowed by the circumstances of their Amateur Cup exit. And press speculation close to the semi-final suggested The Gunners could find themselves kicked out of a second tournament:

> *'As regards the Army Cup, all kinds of rumours are in the air,' said the* Southern Daily Mail. *Should RA lose their appeal, they must be thrown out of the Army Cup. But it's pretty certain that the Army FA will not take RA's professionalism without a protest. It has become customary for army clubs to train systemically for their cup ties, and the FA will doubtless be required to frame another new rule plainly stipulating what training is required.'*

This point was backed up by the authoritative 1906 publication, *Book of Football*:

> *'Towards the end of (1898/99) arose the sensational disqualification of the Portsmouth RA from the Amateur Cup. The lesson was most beneficial; the old rule of seven days limited training was abolished and regiments have since found themselves on a more equal footing.'*

RA had enjoyed good fortunes in the Army Cup. How everyone connected with the club must have wished for some of the previous successes to rub off on a season which had degenerated into chaos. The players must have gone into the crucial semi-final with the 1st Bt South Lancs Rgt buoyed by the news, 24 hours earlier, the club's latest protest about their expulsion would be given another hearing by the FA, coincidentally in Birmingham. Everything looked to be going well for The Gunners against South Lancs in the game as they weathered the Preston side's vigorous play to settle down and put Mayflower under pressure in their opponents' goal. He proved capable of dealing with everything until Hanna's capital centre allowed Brazier to score with a nicely-placed shot.

The half-time lead, though, proved to be no guarantee of a final place for RA. South Lancs got their reward for pressuring The Gunners severely when Larkin equalized. RA came back strongly but could not force a winner before the 90 minutes were up. They failed to sustain their efforts and had no answers when South Lancs scored two further goals in extra time. The regiment went on to face the Army Service Corps, 2–0 winners against the Rifles from Cork in the other semi-final.

The result was a surprise and a disappointment to The Gunners. And it was almost the end for their players. A road traffic accident at the start of their journey home left them bruised and shaken, and Harms being admitted to hospital. *The Portsmouth Evening News* gave details of the crash the next day, March 17:

'Contrary to expectations, the RA team were able to leave Birmingham this morning for Portsmouth. They were the victims last night of an alarming incident. While returning from their match at Villa Park, the team and several officers were riding in a char-a-banc. On reaching the boundary, the wheels became locked in the tram-lines and the sudden wrench caused one of the wheels to collapse. The occupants were thrown violently to the ground but, with one exception, they escaped with bruises and severe shaking. An NCO named Harms seemed in a bad way. And he was taken to hospital. It was thought that his pelvis was fractured but an examination showed no bone was broken. By a late train, the team left Birmingham and Harms was sufficiently recovered to undertake the journey.'

Southern League 1898/99 – First Division

	P	W	D	L	F	A	Pts
Southampton	24	15	5	4	54	24	35
Bristol City	24	15	3	6	55	12	33
Millwall Athletic	24	12	6	6	59	35	30
Chatham	24	10	8	6	32	23	28
Reading	24	9	8	7	31	24	26
New Brompton	24	10	5	9	38	30	25
Tottenham Hotspur	24	10	4	10	40	36	24
Bedminster	24	10	4	10	35	39	24
Swindon Town	24	9	5	10	43	49	23
Brighton United	24	9	2	13	37	48	20
Gravesend United	24	7	5	12	42	52	19
Sheppey United	24	5	3	16	23	53	13
Royal Artillery (Portsmouth)	24	4	4	16	17	60	12

Test Matches

Sheppey United	1	1	Thames Ironworks	(Chatham)
Royal Artillery (Portsmouth)	1	4	Cowes	(Southampton)

· C H A P T E R   T W E N T Y - N I N E ·

March 1899 – A Sad Sight

The semi-final was effectively the end of RA as a team of note. They had six games left to play in the Southern League's first division but the Army Cup defeat, allied to the debates in the committee rooms, had crushed the life out of the club. March 18 saw The Gunners return to a Men's Ground raked by a biting cold wind to take on Bristol City in the league. A good attendance, reported to be larger than usual, witnessed a pathetic spectacle for a club recently so proud. *The Portsmouth Evening News*' match report read like an obituary:

'This was a sad sight to see. It marked the end of RA as a force to be reckoned with. The team that had brought soccer success to Portsmouth collapsed against their opponents. One home match, versus Bedminster, is left in the Southern League. Away games are lined up at Sheppey, Bedminster, Reading and the return at Bristol City. RA fared fairly well at first, despite feeling tired and despondent from their Army Cup defeat. They held their own in midfield and, while their attack was not so dangerous, good play by Reilly and Turner combined to foil the visitors. But RA's season was over as they let in three second-half goals.'

The half-time score was 0–0 but the rout began 12 minutes after the break. By the time the second City goal had gone in, after a mistake by Turner, the fight was going out of RA. They lost heart and play was confined to their area as they fell to pieces.

The visitors notched their third, and final, goal as they played around with the once-proud Gunners. The sound of the final whistle was a relief to the stunned crowd. The sense of disbelief was summed up by the *Southern Daily Mail*:

'The spectators could hardly believe their eyes when some of the men merely looked on instead of doubling after their opponents. Training! Why some of the players were not able to raise a gallop. It's perfectly certain the Amateur Cup fiasco has completely upset the players. (After half-time), there was only one team in it and that was not the RA, not by a long way!'

Another defeat followed off the Kent coast – 1–0 to fellow strugglers Sheppey Utd – before Bedminster allowed RA to restore some pride in a Good Friday fixture on the other side of the country.

The home side were reduced to ten men through injury but a win to a team in RA's situation was welcome under any circumstances. Jardine scored the game's only goal from a McGibbon cross in the second-half. Whitehouse, in the Bedminster goal, had rarely seen the ball before the interval once an opening bout of pressure from RA had subsided.

His opposite number, Reilly, had his work cut out on several occasions to keep a clean sheet but he managed to preserve his side's slim lead. The second away victory from their 11th league game on their travels was hailed by the *Portsmouth Times* 'as the best thing The Gunners have done this season'.

March – April 1899
Gunners' Goodbye

RA's next fixture was back in a meeting room. The latest venue was the Queen's Hotel in Birmingham. The FA were staying at the hotel for the England v Scotland game at Aston Villa, where RA had so recently played an Army Cup semi-final. The morning of the April 8 international was spent in a special general meeting of the association debating RA's future – or lack of it. The Gunners were determined to make the most of the last chance to survive. They distributed to the FA's representatives a dossier with full details of the controversial week at Aldeburgh which was under scrutiny. RSM Windrum and Sgt Bonney represented the club to the FA.

The motion under discussion stayed the same, that the week at Aldeburgh and the visit to Crystal Palace had made RA's players professionals. Referees' representative C.D. Crisp, of Ryde, stated the case on RA's behalf and moved the following resolution:

> *'That this specially convened general meeting of the FA finds that sufficient evidence has not been adduced whereby the members of RA (Portsmouth) football team should have been declared professionals.'*

A Mr Grant, of Blackburn Rovers, briefly seconded the motion. Their pleas for the verdict of the Amateur Cup emergency committee, backed on appeal, to be overturned were to no avail. A discussion ended with a repeat of the committee's opinion by 72 votes to 52.

It was difficult to imagine on practical grounds alone how the FA could have come to any other conclusion. The Amateur Cup final, which RA had been favourites to reach, had already taken place ten days earlier without them. RA would have gained no consolation from the fact the instigators of their downfall, Harwich and Parkeston, were defeated in their first Amateur Cup final by Stockton by a single goal after having overcome Grimsby All Saints 2–1 in the semi-final.

The decision which extinguished the hope that RA might have a future was not without its controversial aspect, of course. It was reported by the *Southern Daily Mail* that justification for The Gunners' week away was found in a search of the FA's minute book after the close of the meeting which had decided the fate of the Artillerymen.

A minute dated eight years earlier ruled that certain training expenses for amateurs should be allowed, though why the search was left so late was not reported in the press. RA's appeal reached the venerable column of *The Times* along with its brief report of the international encounter which followed the meeting as the whole footballing world came alive debating the issue. The FA's decision re-ignited the fury of the *Portsmouth Times*, loyal as ever to the cause of The Gunners, to new levels on April 15:

> *'It's the old, old story of the innocent being made to suffer for the sins of the guilty. That a lot of underhand professionalism is going on is common knowledge and so, because they have done*

their best to train and thus improve their play, the RA are dropped upon as the victims. Even if a technical offence had been committed, the punishment was out of all proportion to the crime. But, under the circumstances, it's simply outrageous and says little for the common-sense of the powers that be. (RA) were getting too dangerous and had to be squashed while the pseudo amateur civilians laugh in their sleeves at the gullibility of the FA. Reinstatement is, of course, impossible this season, and I am very much afraid that the death knell of The Gunners has been sounded. It's a cruel piece of injustice but what's been done can't be undone.'

A more relaxed and optimistic line was persisted in by the *Southern Daily Mail*:

'That the RA club will continue to exist is a foregone conclusion and that it will continue to flourish is the hope of all real sportsmen, who have watched its passage through the storm and stress of the past few weeks.'

But the newspaper stressed that nothing definite had been decided by the officials of The Gunners beyond the fielding of a reserve side in the remaining Southern League games.

It was, indeed, a second team, untainted by the charge of professionalism, which took to the field in front of a large crowd on April 8 to fulfil RA's final home league fixture against Bedminster as the impact of the FA's decision was seen within hours.

Like lambs to the slaughter, was the *Portsmouth Evening News'* depiction of the game. But players such as Sutherland, Taylor and McBirnie, with no experience of the Southern League, came close to snatching a point off the visitors, aided by Bedminster's poor shooting.

It took until the final five minutes before the Bristol team managed to take the lead they had threatened so long. A slip by RA's number ten, Woods, let in Copeland. He instantly took advantage to beat Harms, more usually a full-back in previous seasons, with a good shot. Until then, the stand-in keeper had given a brilliant display between the posts but that was the moment when his makeshift side's luck ran out.

Bedminster's wretched shooting, the brilliant form of the three RA backs, plus Harms's amazing saves, were in the past. RA collapsed as Bennett added a second goal just before the final whistle. It was a fitting result, if a tough one on The Gunners.

The Royal Oak ground of Harwich & Parkeston, where RA's downfall began.

Any hopes raised by the performance that RA could, somehow, survive as a formidable outfit in keeping with their past exploits were totally in shreds by half-time of the following game. Bedminster's neighbours, Bristol City, inflicted the damage at their St John's Lane home. Those opening 45 minutes saw Stevenson gain a hat-trick as City romped to a 4–1 lead.

He opened the scoring after ten minutes. RA's team of reserves were three goals down before they could muster a reply. The second-half continued in the same manner as City sought to finish runners-up to Southampton by winning 6–1. Meanwhile, RA's official reserve side had finished exactly halfway in the US League of eight sides. Their record was: P13 W5 D3 L5 F23 A26 Pts 13.

This showing at least made it easier for the club to field 11 strong second XI players to see out their Southern League fixtures at Reading. Another brilliant display by Harms was unable to prevent the inevitable defeat – 5–0. A lot of hard-thinking had been carried out by the club in between matches as they tried to discover a way out of the situation they had been placed in by the FA's rulings.

But the one escape route that seemed open was determinedly shunned by RA. The option on offer to The Gunners was to sign professional forms as directed by the FA. They would then have to ask the Army FA for permission to remain in the military service as a professional outfit for the rest of the rapidly closing season. An application for the FA to reinstate the club as amateurs would follow on May 1.

As a survival tactic, it apparently had its share of obstacles but it could have worked if the club had been willing to try. They weren't. Sgt Bonney explained that to attempt it would be tantamount to declaring themselves to be something they weren't. Although they had been affirmed as professionals, they were equally adamant they were nothing of the sort. It was all a matter of principle.

But Sgt Bonney revealed RA did intend to apply in May for the reinstatement of the players condemned to the wilderness by the FA's judgement. By this method, and the use of reserves until the season's end, it was hoped The Gunners could carry on.

Whatever happened, they had no hope of avoiding the end of season battle against relegation. Just one test match would be held between each of the bottom two clubs in the Southern League's first division and the top teams of the second division's London and south west sections at the end of the first season in which the lower flight had been split into two groupings.

That was unlucky for RA. For the team sitting proudly at the top of the south west section, and whom league officials had decreed RA must meet in the winner takes all contest, was none other than Cowes. The side from across the Solent had already convincingly dumped a full-strength Gunners team out of the English Cup, after a replay, earlier in the season.

They could also go into the test match backed by a 100 per cent league record. They had scored 58 goals and conceded just eight during their ten wins. If only, The Gunners must have been thinking, they could have been drawn to play Thames Ironworks, later West Ham United, who had topped the London section, instead of a side against whom they were jinxed.

The reserve/first XI's displays had done nothing to inspire confidence the poor fortunes against Cowes could be overcome. They did little better when the sides met in the crucial game in late April. The island outfit duly clinched promotion with a convincing 4–1 victory. Two Cowes goals in five second-half minutes destroyed what little hope a 2–0 half-time deficit had offered The Gunners. Their consolation goal from full back Leach was too little, too late.

RA were relegated after just one season among the top football outfits in the south. Their league record, excluding the Warmley matches, made depressing reading:

P24 W4 D4 L16 F17 A60 Pts 12.

15. 1899.

FOOTBALL

After several weeks of suspense the R.A. at last know their fate, as the Council of the F.A. have upheld the decision of the Emergency Committee declaring them professionals. The facts are to well known to need repetition; it is the old old story of the innocent being made to suffer for the sins of the guilty. That a lot of under-hand professionalism is going on is common knowledge, and so, because they have done their best to train and thus improve their play, the R.A. are dropped upon as the victims. Even if a technical offence had been committed the punishment would be out of all proportion to the crime, but under the circumstances it is simply outrageous and says little for the fairness or commonsense of the powers that be.

"Gentlemen" players may live in luxury at the expense of the home clubs they visit and even get a guarantee of £2,000 for a six weeks' tour in South Africa, and nothing is said; like certain "amateur" cricketers I could mention, these men have no more claim to that title than, say, Harwich have. What a sensation an investigation into the books of some of these precious

The Portsmouth Times reacted with fury to the FA's final finding of professionalism against RA.

They had won the least games in the first division, scored the fewest goals and conceded the most. Only Sheppey Utd, with 13 points, kept The Gunners company at the foot of the table.

There was then a gap of six points until the safety of the third from bottom team, Gravesend. That had been a divide which RA seldom seemed capable of bridging and which the FA's decision had turned into an abyss of ambition. The Gunners were consigned to oblivion.

Summing up the ill-fated campaign, the *Portsmouth Evening News* showed restraint in commenting it had been a season of two halves. A series of disasters had overtaken The Gunners in the latter part of the season to cause the sequence of lamentable results which led to them possessing the wooden spoon, it said.

The newspaper broke down the campaign to give RA nine games in the second half of the season of which they lost seven and won two. Even more damning were the goals statistics – three scored and 25 conceded. The newspaper stated one bright spot to illuminate the months of gloom had been the progress of the reserves. Brazier, Turner, McNeil and Coutts had all sprung from the ranks of the second XI over the years and had shown brilliant form in the first team, especially Turner.

Matt (or Mick) Reilly cuts his usual dominant figure as Pompey's first team lined up for the photographer before the start of the club's debut season of 1899/1900. The famous goalkeeper was in the middle of the back row with his fearsome moustache making him instantly recognisable. His reputation, which was based on his constant match-winning displays for RA, continued to gain momentum with the new professional club Pompey until the end of 1903/04.
Standing alongside Reilly in that historic photograph was Pompey's more unsung capture from the disintegrating RA team. Harold Turner, first left in the back row, achieved a feat his illustrious team-mate for a decade was unable to claim. He played in the Football League, albeit for only one season, with New Brighton.

Even events outside of RA's control had gone against the club. The three points they had gained in the fixtures against Warmley counted for nothing with the Bristol club's collapse when player power proved unsustainable. It was a condition RA were also close to. *The Portsmouth Evening News* could see no real prospects for the team:

'What may be the future of RA, it's hard to say. The probabilities are that next year will see them forced into a "back seat" role by the Portsmouth professional team and engaging in Army Cup and suchlike mild diversions.'

Only a few months earlier, that had been the new professional club's destiny. As an assessment, it gained broad agreement from the still fuming *Portsmouth Times*:

'The FA's decision was entirely unjustifiable, a fact which they apparently realise now… that a new rule is being framed which will meet such a case as the RAs. The Gunners have been the victims of a mixture of jealousy on the one part and stupidity on the other. The past season has been the most successful and the most disastrous for the RA. It has been successful in as much as the RA, though playing against an entirely different class of club to those which they had previously met, have performed in a manner which has won for them the sympathy and admiration of the football world, excepting certain clubs who shall be nameless.'

How Harwich and Dovercourt fans read about the expulsion of RA from the Amateur Cup following the Essex side's protests.

One of those outfits, Harwich and Parkeston, had ruined The Gunners' status as favourites for the Amateur and Army cups with their 'bolt from the blue' protest, the newspaper continued.

'For five seasons, the RA have been practically the sole caterers for the Portsmouth footballing public, and right notably have they fulfilled the task. Look at the difference between when they started and now. Then, a 1,500 gate was wonderful. Now anything under double that number is poor. See there what a vastly improved standard of play now prevails: truly, Portsmouth owes much to the plucky soldiers who have, from a humble start, gained a place among the best teams in the south and earned themselves undying fame. Whatever may happen, their memory will always be cherished by the footballing public; the fame of The Blossoms will go down to posterity.'

An Irish Idol

O ne Gunner whose name was certainly destined for posterity already had his future assured. Gnr Reilly's name was foremost among the first batch of signings announced by Pompey secretary and manager Frank Brettell. The goalkeeper was set to leave the army soon after the 1898/99 season ended. It was widely agreed the new club had made the best choice of custodian possible in taking on the idol of local football supporters.

'*Reilly is too well-known locally to need much introduction,*' the *Portsmouth Evening News* commented, '*And is undoubtedly one of the best goalkeepers the army has ever produced. This has been noticed not only by Portsmouth but by several other well-known local clubs who have been desperate to secure his services.*' The goalkeeper presented a solid sight to opposing forwards at 5ft 10½ in tall and weighing more than 13 stones. He was making his move into professional football at the age of 24. His prowess at the sport was all the more remarkable because his initial introduction came when he entered the army.

But a club v. country clash cost the most famous Gunner the true international recognition his talents deserved. Reilly's two appearances for Ireland could have been more than doubled if Pompey had been prepared to release their top custodian whenever his country wanted him.

Of the two internationals he did play, it was the second in which Reilly – or Ginger or Mickey to his many fans – starred which showed his position among the top rank of keepers around the turn of the 20th century.

The Times waxed lyrical in its praise of his display in the March 22, 1902, game against England at the Belfast site of the N.E. Agricultural Association, with its coarse turf made slippery by rain. Reilly earned the praise in spite of his country's single-goal defeat in front of 12,000 spectators to a side which contained the legendary forward Steve Bloomer, of Derby County, and Nottingham Forest's top back James Iremonger.

The newspaper commented:

Matt Riley

'*With the ball constantly in their opponents' half, the England forwards should certainly have scored more than once but, apart from the difficulty of controlling the ball, they had a splendid goal keeper to beat, Reilly of Portsmouth, who was at his best.*'

Reilly's superb show, allied to England's poor shooting, meant he remained unbeaten until five minutes from the end when Settle shot low and hard just out of his reach. Ireland struggled hard to save the game but their defeat had been effectively decided earlier when Milne missed a penalty to waste his country's chance of a first win over England. *The Portsmouth*

Times was similarly impressed by Ginger's contribution to the match. He had distinguished himself, it said:

> '*Reilly gave a good display in goal for Ireland on Saturday and the narrow margin by which his country was defeated was largely down to his skill and pluck.*'

But the keeper's appearance had been initially in doubt. *The Portsmouth Evening News* of March 8 warned Reilly's fans he might be unable to take up the selectors' offer:

> '*Portsmouth followers of the game – and they number their thousands now – will be glad to see that Reilly, the Portsmouth goalie, has been chosen to play for Ireland. The honour is well deserved, though it's doubtful if the directors can spare the nimble Mickey for, on the Saturday fixed for the match, Pompey are due to entertain Swindon Town at Fratton Park and Southern League points are priceless right now.*'

In the event, George Harris took Reilly's place to help Pompey to keep a clean sheet as they won 4–0 in another step towards their first Southern League championship. Reilly's second international came two years after he first wore his country's colours.

But even that initial appearance was put in doubt by Pompey's reluctance to release their star player for the fixture with England. News of his selection in the *Portsmouth Evening News* of March 7, 1900, was tempered with the warning he could forego his date with his country because of his club's fixture in the Southern League at Gravesend Utd:

> '*Reilly's numerous friends will be glad to know that the talented goalkeeper's abilities have been recognised. That he will do credit to his native country goes without saying. Mr Brettell (Pompey's manager) intends to make every effort to obtain a substitute for Reilly…*'

Hopes of securing former England international, the Rev G.B. Raikes, who had beaten Reilly to first place in a top goalkeeper of the south poll four years earlier, for the Gravesend match were foiled. Pompey's custodian was only able to win his first cap thanks to the willingness of his former RA team-mate Harms to replace him between the posts.

In his only appearance for Pompey, Harms was given a hard time by the home forwards in the opening minutes but he kept a clean sheet to help his temporary side to a 1–0 win.

Meanwhile, Reilly was making his Irish debut at the Lansdowne Ground in Dublin's first hosting of an international fixture. The match was the first international out of four, the second of which was 30 years later, to feature two Pompey players on opposing sides. In the England team on March 17, 1900, facing Reilly was Danny Cunliffe, the demon Pompey goal-getter, as he was described by the *Portsmouth Times*.

The forward had scored twice in a 4–4 draw in the English north v south trial game to earn his selection. He played well in England's 2–0 defeat of the Irish. But the plaudits, as usual, went to Reilly. In the eyes of the *Portsmouth Times*:

> '*Reilly gave a magnificent display and had much to do with the smallness of the score against his country. Some of his clearances savoured positively of the miraculous and Ireland can congratulate herself on having at last recognised the claims of one of the finest custodians in the kingdom.*'

The recognition was followed by a long gap in international appearances outside of the Irish selectors' control. They chose Ginger three times in 1900/01 only for Pompey to refuse to release him from their Southern and

Western League campaigns. One of the internationals Reilly had to miss was the February 23, 1901, match with Scotland.

His presence was desperately needed as Ireland slumped to an 11–0 defeat, their heaviest in games between the two countries. Swindon were again Pompey's opponents on the day of the international and Reilly travelled with his club to the County Ground to help record a 3–0 win. What he thought of being denied his true international recognition can only be guessed at.

But the *Portsmouth Times* was, nonetheless, proud he was good enough to be considered for his country as the newspaper recapped on the season:

> *'Three times this season Reilly has had to refuse international caps to play for the club to which he has rendered such splendid service. Reilly has been before the sporting public of this town for seven years or so and has attained a popularity only in accordance with his merits. All he knows of the game, he has learnt in this town and we are all the more proud of Ginger for that reason.'*

A week later saw a crowd estimated at 1,500 attend Reilly's testimonial, Pompey's first. Fellow Southern League side West Ham Utd provided the opposition at Fratton Park on April 28, 1901. The East Londoners entered into the spirit of the occasion by playing for just their travelling expenses as they rounded off the season.

The fixture took quick advantage of a rule change by the FA. It had decided to allow players a benefit game every five years or when they retired. The game lived up to the prediction of success by the *Portsmouth Evening News*: 'His many friends, civilian and military, should rally round the old Artilleryman on that occasion, and see he benefits materially'. More than 2,000 tickets were sold before the game to give a level of interest double some of Pompey's gates for their home Western League fixtures. The only aspect which spoiled the occasion was the goal the Hammers scored past Reilly after just ten minutes. Radcliffe's fast shot gave the keeper no chance.

Reilly's colleagues – Lewis and Marshall – hit back to enable Pompey to end the game as 2–1 winners. However, the keeper almost never signed for the club at all. A host of sides were aware of the fact he was due to end his army service at the end of the 1898/99 season. Football League champions Aston Villa and several Southern League clubs were among them.

But his inclusion among the initial batch of signings by Pompey's manager Brettell re-assured their fans about their immediate prospects. *The Southern Daily Mail* welcomed Reilly's commitment to the Fratton Park outfit:

> *'Some of the principal clubs in the country were anxious for the popular "Ginger's" signature but, fortunately for the new concern, he was persuaded to remain at the scene of his many triumphs, and in this department Portsmouth will be second to no club.'*

Reilly was a virtual ever-present during Pompey's first five seasons in which he enabled the club to make the best possible start to their life. They were never lower than fourth in the Southern League. A debut performance of second place was followed by the league championship in 1901/02 in the middle of a three-year reign as Western League champions. A tribute from the *Portsmouth Times* on the occasion of Reilly's marriage in September 1900 best summed up his influence on the club:

> *'His magnificent goalkeeping, combined with his unfailing good humour and pluck have made him the idol of the local football public. And it's not too much to say that even on other grounds, where rivalry runs high, he is an established favourite.'*

That rivalry was seen only too clearly in one of Reilly's last appearances for Pompey. Swindon once more loomed large in his playing career as the January 30, 1904, Southern League fixture at the Wiltshire outfit was interrupted by crowd trouble.

Reilly was incensed at being bombarded with clinker by the home fans and, in a repeat of the fracas in the RA versus Wycombe Wanderers game seven years earlier, took matters into his Irish hands and hit one of the supporters. His loss of temper resulted in a two-match suspension.

Three months later, and Reilly played his last game for Pompey. It ended in a 2–0 defeat away to Plymouth Argyle in the Southern League. His career at Fratton Park amounted to 206 league games, 21 cup ties and 31 friendlies. He moved on to Scottish first division side Dundee.

He continued to run the Duke of Devonshire pub in Albert Road, Southsea, which he took over in January 1903, past his retirement from the game. He then moved to his native Dublin, where he had been born in the Donnybrook district. He still kept some links with Pompey. He travelled over with his wife and family to see the club face Manchester City in the 1934 FA Cup final.

He sent before him his best wishes and a silver horseshoe with the words 'Play up Pompey', which he had helped to inspire. He bound a sprig of white heather to the good luck symbol and in between the horns was a painted shamrock. The item was placed on the mantelpiece in the Fratton Park boardroom.

Ill-health stopped Reilly from making his planned appearance at Pompey's golden jubilee celebrations in November 1948. His influence on the formative years of the club and football in the city was spelt out to celebrating supporters. "Ranger", of the *Football Mail*, called him 'outstanding in his day and generation':

'The Donnybrook Bhoy, as he was called by his admiring fellow Gunners, came to the front with RA and dawned upon the Portsmouth football world as a positive genius. Weight, good temper, a sunny Irish disposition, calmness and strength were Reilly's strong points and he, of course, innovated the bouncing out principle. This would not have been safe for most goalkeepers but, with the big Irishman, it generally paid.'

He began the technique early in his RA career much to the bemusement of supporters at grounds where The Gunners visited. The November 11, 1895, game at Bristol South End reported in the *Portsmouth Evening News* was a typical example:

'Reilly, the clever keeper of RA, quite surprised the people of Bristol on Saturday. His well-known tactics of running a considerable distance with the ball and dropping the leather on the ground had never before been witnessed in the district.'

Home supporters had a good look at the tactic when Reilly turned out for RA on April 12, 1897, when they played a charity game for the Portsmouth FA mayor's fund. The match report read:

'Reilly gave a pretty exhibition of his powers and patting the ball out, dodging until he got a chance to throw it away. Reilly apparently was in humorous mood and caused roars of laughter by the way he dodged with the ball and cheered.'

The goalkeeper – a 'fine looking moustachioed Irishman', according to contemporary accounts – died at Donnybrook on December 9, 1954. He was aged 80. A brief obituary in the *Portsmouth Evening News* included this tribute:

'Many of the club's older supporters who recall the Pompey side of Southern League days remember him as an outstanding personality.'

Reilly was the last of The Gunners to turn out for Pompey.

From the Gunners to Pompey

He was originally joined at Fratton Park by his RA team-mate Turner. The right-back had been a sound performer for The Gunners and possessed a nice turn of speed. A former reserve player, he had been one of the few successes of the stressful final season. His new manager was convinced he had the potential to develop a lot further. Brettell believed Turner's absolutely fearless nature and ability to seldom make mistakes with his feet could turn him into one of the best backs in the south when he was faced with taking on top class opponents.

Turner stayed for one season before a knee injury caused Pompey to release him. He joined New Brighton, of the Football League's second division and made light of his ailment by appearing in the Cheshire side's best, and last, season of a short stay in the league.

A return to the south coast brought him back to Fratton Park to re-sign in the summer of 1901. A further 52 appearances were made alongside Reilly in the next two seasons. Turner played for Pompey in a total of 58 league games, seven cup fixtures and 31 friendlies. His final appearance for the club was on March 11, 1903, when he lined up against QPR.

Regimental Sergeant Major Fred Windrum, who was the driving force behind the formation of three leading football clubs of the Victorian era. He was RA's treasurer and trainer and moved on to join the board of directors at Fratton Park. He left Portsmouth about a year later to help to establish Plymouth Arygle. He ended his working life with the Royal Artillery at Woolwich. His Army obituary failed to mention his remarkable record.

Two other players briefly completed the contingent of ex-Gunners at Fratton Park. Harms made just the one appearance for the first team in a competitive fixture – at Gravesend as the stand-in keeper for Reilly – while Hanna also had just a single game to his credit. That was in the Southern District Combination at home to Millwall.

RA's links with Pompey continued for longer off the pitch than they did on it with Sgt Bonney and RSM Windrum as directors. Sgt Bonney's connections with Fratton Park continued well into the 20th Century.

He had already retired from the army when he stepped down from the board in 1904, around the same time as Reilly left for Dundee, to become Pompey's third manager. He guided the club to the runners-up spot in the Southern League and 3rd in the Western League in 1906/07. He went one place better in the Western League the following year with a repeat runners-up performance.

Under his control, Pompey also scored a memorable English Cup triumph against Manchester United in 1906/07 and embarked on their first continental tour at the end of that season. But his reign ended on an unhappy note in 1910/11 with Pompey's first relegation. They had finished bottom of the Southern League's first division. A financial crisis loomed as well.

Sgt Bonney's time as manager was over – and the RA thread which had run continuously through Pompey's early years disappeared with him. He had greatly outlasted RSM Windrum's involvement on the board. That ended after just a year or so as a director.

He was commissioned as a District Officer and posted to Plymouth. His promotion, at the time of Reilly's first international in March 1900, delighted the local press. One report read:

'He is well known in Portsmouth athletic circles, and football especially, owes its popularity as much to him as to any man in the town. He was one of the principal supporters of the old RA team and, since the formation of the new Portsmouth club, has been one of the most popular directors.'

The Portsmouth Times match report of the game which led to Harwich & Parkeston's leading role in the success of Portsmouth FC.

The new District Officer went on to play a major role in the development of Plymouth Argyle. He retired from the military in 1920 as a Lt-Colonel while he was running the RA Mess at Woolwich. He undertook the role from 1915 until his death in April 1952, a month short of his 89th birthday.

By then, the Portsmouth club he had played such a prominent part in establishing had celebrated its golden jubilee in November 1948 in the best of health. His part as a director in the formation, along with Sgt Bonney, was acknowledged in the official 50th anniversary handbook of 1948. The publication stated about the pair:

'…both of whom gained intimate knowledge of first-class football and its management through their association with RA. Both were astute and whole-hearted enthusiasts and their election to the directorate was an advantage beyond question.'

RSM Windrum also briefly featured in the newspaper coverage of the golden jubilee as part of the re-awakening of interest in RA's influential exploits. Captain R.W. Gregg (Rtd), from Fareham, told the *Football Mail*'s readers of his memories of RSM Windrum and Sgt Bonney as football correspondent "Ranger" recounted:

'His (Cpt Gregg's) father, the late J.W. Gregg, was for ten years, 1895–1905, the Regimental Quarter Master Sergeant at Clarence Barracks. He often related the achievements of RA to his son, himself too young to see this famous team play. Cpt Gregg says he clearly remembers RSM Windrum and Sgt Bonney, who was the master tailor.'

The anniversary celebrations also contained an echo of the game which enabled the Portsmouth club to immediately occupy the top footballing spot in the town from RA. In among the Football League championship form being shown a place was found for a representative of Harwich and Parkeston.

The Harwich and Dovercourt Standard twice referred to the occasion. Its account of November 26, 1948, reported:

'Harwich and Parkeston FC will be one of the few amateur clubs represented at the jubilee celebration of Portsmouth FC this weekend. The mayor (and football club chairman) Cllr E. Grant is making the long trip to the south in order to represent the club that was largely responsible for the formation of the Portsmouth professional side 50 years ago.'

· C H A P T E R T H I R T Y - T H R E E ·

Oblivion Beckons

But as Pompey were set on the course to such a thriving future, RA were doomed. The new club was willingly accepted into the Southern League by the league's members as expected because none of Pompey's players – Reilly and Turner apart – had been poached from them. The remainder of Pompey's early players were the result of Mr Brettell's scouting in the north of England. The vote took place on May 29, 1899, at the league's annual meeting at the Rainbow Tavern in London's Fleet Street. The contrast in fortunes between Pompey and RA was vast. The new club was among five clubs accepted into the first division of the league. RA's future was dismissed in a single sentence in reports of the meeting:

'It was noted that RA, having been beaten by Cowes in the test match, had retired.'

The US League would also be missing RA Reserves the next season. No application was made by the club to take part. But The Gunners' remarkable, if brief, impact on football was still apparent. Just before Pompey's players were due to report for pre-season training in mid-July, the Portsmouth FA's annual meeting paid rather more respect to RA's passing.

The association's members firmly put the credit with The Gunners for creating the town's burgeoning interest in football. They agreed the side's form and their membership of the Southern League had provided powerful opportunities to generate a lot of enthusiasm, laid sound footings to develop the game and placed Portsmouth on a par with other prominent football centres. But in spite of the FA's reinstatement of RA's players, it was too late to fight on. Reilly and Turner signed for the new professional club and made their debuts in Pompey's Southern League curtain-raiser at Chatham. They had faced three of their former team-mates a week earlier at Fratton Park in a public trial of the new Pompey team versus the reserves.

Sgt Harms was in his new-found position of goal for the second team. In front of him were Smith at number seven and Hanna at number four. Fully 5,000 people watched the game and saw good play by Harms restrict the first team to a two-goal win. The RA connection was strengthened by the presence of Sgt Bonney as referee. He also remained as the Portsmouth representative on the Hampshire FA.

In keeping with the clubs' respective destinies, as Fratton Park was opened, one of RA's usual venues was closed to football. The popularity of The Gunners, and the surge in interest they had generated in football, had combined to wear out the Officers' Ground. The effect on the turf had been particularly noted during the cricket season which had just ended.

The only solution felt by the ground's operators was to ban football for the entire 1899/1900 season to allow the cricket ground to be completely relaid. No such renewal of RA was to take place. Irish international Hanna, the club's captain, had joined Reilly and Turner at Fratton Park, alongside RSM Windrum and Sgt Bonney. Their absence – coupled with the Army FA's newly strict rules and the demands on the army of the Boer War in South Africa – meant RA's days as a playing force were over.

They did survive, however – in spite of the popular belief Pompey's formation signalled the total demise of The Gunners. But the circumstances initially were much reduced from their previous glories. October 1899 found them away to Ryde in a friendly. McNeil remained in the side to score one of The Gunners' goals as they stumbled to a 7–2 defeat. Walsh netted the other.

The ever-loyal *Portsmouth Times* hoped the match was a prelude to an RA team of the future:

> *'If somebody could be found to take the club in hand there's no reason why the army team should not be re-established, for they have plenty of good material to fill the places of some of the players who have left. Of course, they can't hope to regain their old position in the football world, but they could run a team which should worthily represent the corps in the army and local cups next season.'*

Another friendly between the sides took place five months later, at the end of the following March. It ended in an even worse defeat for The Gunners. Four goals down at half-time, they stumbled to a 9–0 hiding on the Isle of Wight. The team on the wrong end of that scoreline: Griffen, Palmer, Peach, Hayhurst, Gomley, Smith, Harrison, Walton, Jardine, Houston, Russell was far removed from the line-up which had taken RA to the heights.

Matt Reilly and Barry Turner visited Chatham's Maidstone Ground once with RA, on October 29, 1899. They left on the wrong end of a 5-0 scoreline. They returned 11 months later for Portsmouth's first game in the Southern League and experienced a happier time. The new club got off to a good start with a 1-0 win. The ground remains in its original site, next to a cemetery on one of the main roads into Chatham, though the investment of funds has resulted in a modern clubhouse for the 1990s.

RA Revival

RA were undaunted by the two heavy setbacks and reformed for the 1900/01 season to make a renewed impact – but only on the parochial football scene. They entered the Hampshire Senior League and the US League as well as the two local cups. Their opponents were the likes of RMA, Rifle Depot and HMS Excellent to take them back to the services set-up where they had started just six years earlier. The first hint that The Gunners had been formally revived appeared with a match result in the *Portsmouth Times* of September 22. RA had been beaten 3–0 at East Cowes Victoria in the preceding week. The middle of October brought the news RA were among the eight members of the first division of a US League also presumed in local footballing circles to be finished but kept going by the enthusiasm of QMS Line.

RA returned to competitive fixtures convincingly thanks to a 6–1 US League win at RA Hilsea on October 24. In hailing the resurrected side, the *Portsmouth Times* reported it seemed like the clock had been turned back:

'The members of the famous old team to turn up were Harms, Phillips, Harper, Coleman, Walsh, Cook and Jardine and when they have had a little more practice they will make a good many of the clubs sit up. At present, one or two of the garrison gunners are not very fit. Cook, who shot three goals, has not lost his old shooting powers, while Walsh and Jardine were also prominent in this line.'

But the famous names from the past still left RA firmly in the shadow of Portsmouth FC's limelight. The only quality consistent with the team of the former seasons was the ability to court controversy. Late October brought the first rude reminder RA were no more than members of the local footballing scene for those still loyal followers who allowed gates at the Men's Ground to be described as 'a large crowd'.

A 4–2 defeat against HMS Excellent in the US League found RA condemned by two spot kicks in spite of having the better of the play:

'...general opinion being in favour of the once famous Gunners,' wrote the *Portsmouth Times. 'Play was very vigorous, if not to say rough and two penalties were given against the soldiers.'*

The Hampshire Senior Cup took the soldiers across the Solent to Ryde for a 3–1 first round defeat to wipe out any hopes in that competition. A similar fate was in store in the Portsmouth Senior Cup, two weeks later on November 27. The Gunners went down 4–1 at home to Naval Depot, or US Depot, depending on which match report was read.

Players 1900–1901

Benson
Cook/Cooke Gnr
Coleman, H.C. Sgt
Dodds
Davey
Haxton/Huxton, Micky
Hayhurst/Hayhunt
Harms, H.R. Cpl
Harper Gnr
Harrison, E.
Hendry
Hill, William Gnr
Jardine, D. Gnr
Moss
MacMillan
McNeil, J. Gnr
Parmer/Palmer
Phillips, Davie Gnr
Simpson
Sutherland
Savage
Walsh/Walch, Paddy Cpl

In between those setbacks came news of three Gunners. Haxton and McNeil returned from the Boer War to help their side to a 6–0 win in the US League over 20th Co RA. Haxton – along with Cook – was also at the centre of an intriguing item in the *Portsmouth Times* as November continued:

> *'Two popular favourites of the past, now once again disporting themselves with RA, Haxton and Cook, have been reinstated as amateurs by the FA who have certainly not hurried themselves in the matter considering the fact both men came up from the reserves about a year ago. Haxton had just signed on for QPR and Cook went with Eastleigh.'*

Neither player was among those who made the infamous trip to Aldeburgh, but no reason was given about the need to declare then anew as amateurs. Similarly, both continued to appear for RA in 1900/01, despite the mention in the report of the other clubs. Another famous player, Phillips, also returned to The Gunners' fold for the cup defeat by the Naval Depot, after he had appeared in the season's opening fixture.

And so, what was to become RA's farewell season, continued. They were certainly good enough to compete at the local level which used to be the domain of their reserves. The Gunners had played their way to the top of the US League as February began. They had gained 11 points out of a possible 16, according to the *Portsmouth Evening News*, helped by such home results as the six-goal beatings inflicted on 20th Co RA and RMLI.

The Gunners were still in pole position a month later, having taken their points total from ten games to 14, with a 5–1 drubbing of HMS Excellent in a top of the table clash helping to cement their place. RA stayed in contention for the championship by winning at least two of their remaining fixtures as the season closed. One of those victories – given as 8–1 or 7–1 in the newspapers – was notable for more than the result.

RA's opponents, RA Hilsea, brought the March 20 fixture to a premature close. The newspapers were agreed on that point at least. *The Southern Daily Mail* commented:

> *'But towards the finish a singular incident happened. The Hilsea men disagreed with a decision given by Mr Apps, the referee, and all of them, excepting two forwards, walked off the field.'*

The Portsmouth Times added:

> *'The RA made hacks of the Hilsea Gunners… but the latter left the field two minutes before the finish because they disagreed with a decision of the referee. There is trouble in store for them.'*

RA's much reduced stature against the might of the creditable performances of Portsmouth FC in the Southern and Western Leagues was reflected in the total lack of publicity about the final position of The Gunners in the US League. Three years before, the team from the US Men's Ground had received prominent coverage in all the local newspapers.

Now they did not merit a mention in any of the three leading publications in the town who vied with each other to give their readers the most up-to-date and comprehensive facts about the new club as a new era for football dawned in Portsmouth to tie in with the passing of the Victorian era in society generally. The gaslight world of the former Queen was fading fast and taking RA at the same time.

But The Gunners' occupation of the US League's prime position during the 1900/01 season seemed to be only temporary. RMA, who had defeated The Artillerymen 3–1 in November, had a maximum points haul from their four games. Their goal difference of 20–4 was also much better than RA's figures of F21 A16. HMS Excellent were another side well placed for the top spot. They had eight points out of ten.

But the outcome of The Gunners' efforts in the Hampshire Senior League is known. They finished as the runners-up of the five members. The reduced nature of the competition, compared to RA's previous experiences, was shown by their final playing record in the official figures: P8 W2 D5 L1 F7 A6 Pts 9.

Five years earlier, they had recorded ten victories to earn the runners-up spot. Perhaps more consolation was to be gained from their undefeated performances against the reserve sides of Pompey and Saints.

The Gunners took three out of the four points from their encounters with the second string of Portsmouth FC. Their victory came in the February 23 fixture at Fratton Park before 'a decent gate'. *The Portsmouth Times* noted:

'As in the old days, the Gunners' principal point is defence and half-backs, their backs and goalkeeper took a devil of a beating. Lewis put Pompey Reserves 1–0 up. Play was more even in the second-half with Moss (in the RA goal) having to do most of the goalkeeping but just when the reserves looked to have the points secured Cook scored twice to give his side the verdict.'

The teams' initial meeting at the Men's Ground, in early January, drew this comment from the newspaper:

'During the first half, The Gunners did their share of aggressive work but for the rest of the game the civilians attacked continuously and deserved to score. It was then that the good qualities of the RA defence were seen and Haxton, Moss, Leach and Palmer proved more than a match for the Pinks' forwards.'

The Hampshire Telegraph agreed RA had played well:

'It should be said that they had most of the game, though the result was an injustice to the civilians.'

The Gunners' meetings with the second XIs of the Saints were a month apart, in March and April. Both ended in 1–1 draws to confirm RA's reputation at the draw specialists of the Hampshire Senior League. The first of the clashes was again dominated by the Artillerymen's rearguard. Walsh, at centre-half, was said by the *Portsmouth Times* to have been the man of the match. Moss, Palmer, Haxton and Sutherland also did good work in defence. But they were beaten by Cavendish 15 minutes from the end and it took an 85th minute goal by Harrison to secure a point.

The Good Friday return at The Dell on April 5 should have resulted in a win for RA, according to the match report. But 1900/01 closed with the dispiriting news that Coleman, of the forwards, was the only Gunner selected for an Army and Navy team to take on Portsmouth FC at Fratton Park.

The representative team, in contrast, featured four Naval Depot players, three from HMS Excellent and two RMA members. The Gunners were rapidly slipping from view. And, as 1901/02 got underway, the *Portsmouth Times* asked in its edition of September 7:

'The Hampshire Senior League has been expanded and now consists of eight clubs but what's wrong with Naval Depot (the champions) and RA?'

No answer was ever printed.

Hampshire League

1898/99	No entry from Royal Artillery
1899/1900	No entry from Royal Artillery

1900/01	*P*	*W*	*D*	*L*	*F*	*A*	*Pts*
Royal Naval Depot	8	4	3	1	19	7	11
Royal Artillery (Portsmouth)	8	2	5	1	7	6	9
Southampton Res	8	3	2	3	19	11	8
Portsmouth Res	8	3	2	3	17	13	8
Eastleigh Athletic	8	2	0	6	6	31	4

Changed Circumstances

**N**o one better symbolised the change of status of RA than Hanna. A mere 18 months separated his appearance for Ireland, as the first international footballer in Portsmouth, and a place among the fringe players of the new professional club. From leading his country to a 1–0 win against Wales, the fate of The Gunners' captain so soon afterwards was to appear before small crowds at Fratton Park in meaningless friendly fixtures.

Hanna had led RA to four national cup finals, and another with RA (Gosport), to establish the side as being in south-east England's leading group. But matches against the likes of Spurs and Southampton were replaced by turning out to take on Southsea and Brighton United Reserves.

The first hint of Hanna's drastically reduced circumstances came in Portsmouth's initial friendlies as the new club sought to establish itself and its following at the still unnamed Goldsmith Avenue ground. The initial development of the ground had provided an unnerving background for The Gunners as they competed in the Southern League's first division.

Hanna got his spell with his new team off to the best possible start. He was among the scorers in a 2–2 draw which Portsmouth Reserves secured in a trial match against players drawn from the footballing scene in the town. He was named among the half-backs as the reserves lined up for the August 26 friendly in 1899. His colleagues just ahead of the defence were Halliday and Digweed (Hornets).

He was again present on September 1 for a game against a US League XI. It would appear Hanna was still in the army. One of his games for the professionals was accompanied by the initials 'RA' in place of the club names which were often added to the names of his new team-mates.

The reduced nature of Hanna's contribution to the Portsmouth footballing scene was shown by the following article in the *Portsmouth Evening News* a week later which previewed an exhibition game versus Ryde:

> '*In this exhibition match at Ryde on Monday (Sept 11) Pompey will be represented by their full strength, except that Hanna will take the place of Stringfellow at centre half-back.*'

Later that week, it was back to practice games fare for the international. He faced Brighton United Reserves at Fratton Park on September 14 before his play against another US League XI earned a mention in the *Portsmouth Evening News*' match report. In the second half, the newspaper reported:

> '*Hanna again returned the ball to Spicer's end and banged in a splendid shot. The custodian saved. This was the beginning of a prolonged and exciting attack on the goal, which both Spicer and the backs were at their wits' end to repeal. Hanna, however, relieved by shooting over the bar.*'

In between Hanna's matches came some news of his fellow ex-RA players. Jardine and Brazier scored twice each as the 41st Co Southern District RA (SDRA) team clinched a 4–0 win against the 10th Co SDRA side at the USMG. The fine game recorded by the *Portsmouth Evening News* was no doubt helped as well by the presence of Coleman among the 41st Co forwards and Palmer and Leach among the backs. Their opponents included McGibbon and Queenan.

The "peak" of Hanna's career at Fratton Park occurred on November 1 as he appeared in a home Southern District Combination game with Millwall. But his appearance as a half-back was excused in the *Portsmouth Evening News* by the sentence 'six reserves are included in the team because several members are sick'. However, the Artilleryman made the most of his chance by defending grandly in the 3–1 victory. It was not enough for a breakthrough into the Southern League games – a standard he had competed adequately in two years earlier.

It was back to the reserves, instead, three days later for an emphatic ten goal success against Southsea. Next up were Ryde in a friendly and the Royal Marines Artillery in a Portsmouth Senior Cup second round tie at the start of the following month in which Hanna contributed one of the second string's goals in the 5–1 win.

The touring Kaffirs side from South Africa provided the next opposition for Hanna. Another easy win for Portsmouth, 7–3, was recorded. The December 6 match was the last mention of the Irish cap in the affairs of the Fratton Park outfit.

The reason for his absence could lie in newspaper coverage six weeks later which concerned Hanna's more well-known ex-Artilleryman, Reilly. It was reported the goalkeeper had received an army order to join Number 40 Co RA in Ireland as the Boer War intensified. South African place names such as Transvaal and Ladysmith dominated the news pages.

Details of Reilly's call-up by the military reserves broke as Portsmouth prepared for their English Cup tie against the mighty Blackburn Rovers in the biggest game of the south coast club's fledgling career. Fans of the new club were reassured by the *Portsmouth Evening News* they would be still able to see their favourite player between the posts:

'We believe, however, that Pompey will not lose the services of the popular goalkeeper after all, as arrangements have been come to whereby Reilly will be retained for garrison duty at the Portsmouth barracks.'

Hanna's fate and his exploits, again mirror those of RA, in disappearing from public view.

Bombardier
John Hanna, RA

Gone but not Forgotten

I t was as if RA had never existed. A casual observer of the contemporary football scene would be equally unaware of the club's surviving impact on the game. Yet, its influence is as strong as ever, locally and nationally. That impact led to two major developments which concern the laws of the game. Reilly was responsible for the amendment to the rules that limit a keeper's handling of the ball to his penalty area. He had taken advantage of a law adopted in 1888 to permit handling by a keeper anywhere within his own half provided he did not carry the ball more than two steps.

Reilly's induction in Gaelic football, where handling is allowed, is thought to have given him the inspiration for 'patting', or bouncing out, the ball from his goalmouth in line with the FA's rules. The practice gained a lot of attention as Reilly's fame became widely known. Other keepers took up the tactic as news spread.

The FA made it illegal by limiting a keeper's handling to his own area straight after two Scottish goalies had scored in the same match in 1910. The rule has never been changed. Another RA-inspired piece of football legislation is also in place in the late 1990s.

A hundred years ago, in the wake of the battle RA had with the Football Association over the professionalism allegations, the Army FA quickly acted to prevent a repeat by bringing in its first definition of an amateur sportsman. A major revision of its rules included a new clause:

'Any player receiving direct/indirect remuneration of any sort in addition to his third class railway fare and reasonable hotel expenses going to and from a match, should be declared a professional and excluded from the AFA, and any club playing such a player should be excluded from the AFA. A professional should not play for any army team in a match or competition. Training expenses not paid by the players themselves will be considered as remuneration beyond necessary travelling and hotel expenses.'

To clear up any confusion that might have remained, another rule stated:

'No man shall be excused duty for training purposes. Any club found so doing will be disqualified. On no account may a club employ a trainer, other than one borne on the strength of the unit.'

The purpose of the rules still exist, though the detail has been changed to take account of modern soccer. The Army FA's current position, based on guidance from the Football Association, is that any member of the armed forces is banned from holding a contract of employment with any civilian club under the FA's jurisdiction or an affiliated association. The players, however, are encouraged to play civilian football to improve their standards and to be paid for turning out.

Other more physical legacies of RA's yesterday still exist in the Portsmouth of today away from the Fratton Park home of the club's successors. The Gunners' grounds in Burnaby Road and their barracks in the High Street are as much dominant features between Old Portsmouth and the city centre as they were a hundred years past.

The barracks stem from Portsmouth's role as a garrison town being equal to that as a naval base in the 1890s. The need to control the vast British Empire, and to fight the approaching Boer War in South Africa, required a massive military strength. A survey in 1891 showed 2,321 of those soldiers were based in Portsmouth. At least seven major barracks were dotted around the expanding town alone.

Similar establishments existed in the Fareham and Gosport areas. The need for sports facilities to be shared by the services was solved by the reclamation of part of the fortifications network which had surrounded Old Portsmouth and the dam around King's Mill. Clues to the opening of the US Officers' Ground and the US Men's Ground on opposite sides of Burnaby Road can be gathered from various history books.

The first instance of a services sports team being founded was probably the 1862 formation of United Services Rugby Club. This has stayed true to its roots by continuing to play at Burnaby Road, on the site of the former Officers' Ground. The 1907 *Portsmouth and Southsea Guide* informed its readers of the ground's origins:

> 'US Recreation Ground, the embankment of which forms the western end of St Michael's Road, was constructed by government labour, partly from land occupied by the fortifications and partly on the site of the old Milldam.'

Football is still played at the United Services Men's Ground – a century on from RA's demise.

William G. Gates's definitive guide *Portsmouth in the Past*, published in 1927, concurs:

'When the moat was filled in the land was converted into a recreation ground for officers.'

The author said the moat surrounded the Amherst Redoubt, which formed part of the Portsea fortifications. US Rugby Club went nowhere in their first 20 years of using the new ground but a revival in 1882 saw them attracting crowds of 10,000-plus to watch opponents of the calibre of Cardiff and the Australian Wallabies.

Services football was well into its stride by then and RA's formation brought attendances of up to 8,000, usually to the Men's Ground on the venue's southern side. The large scale of the complex was shown by the fact many of RA's services rivals were also based there. But it was The Gunners' surge through the footballing ranks which brought improvements to the ground in its wake.

At least one stand was enlarged and another installed. Match reports also spoke at various times of a Pavilion End, a Railway End and a Town Hall End as the ground became recognised as an established footballing venue. The stadium continued to prosper after the Artillerymen's demise. It was a significant enough destination to warrant a detailed description in that 1907 town guide:

'On the Officers' Ground, county cricket matches take place. There are about a score of tennis courts, accommodation for football, cycling, croquet etc. On the Men's Ground, with the garrison gymnasium at the rear, service cricket and football matches, garrison and naval sports, and military torchlight tattoos take place.'

It is much the same situation nowadays. An armed forces team still plays football on the sports ground to the south of Burnaby Road in the guise of Wessex League side Portsmouth RN. Navy representative matches are also hosted there. A 500-seat stand is the modern equivalent of RA's match facilities. To add to the feeling of *deja vu*, a gymnasium is on the site along with several hockey and minor football pitches.

The ground on the other side of the road continues to host county cricket along with the rugby fixtures. One change is in the name of the location to HMS Temeraire. Another concerns the size of the football crowds attracted there. Three-figure crowds for Portsmouth RN's regional league matches are an exception but the ground did briefly host a leading team in September 1998 when Sunderland used it as their training base between Nationwide League first division fixtures.

Links with the Past

The Men's Ground location was, and still is, a short walk away from RA's headquarters, Cambridge Barracks. The building retains a commanding presence at the junction of High Street, Cambridge Road, St George's Road and Alexandra Road in its contemporary guise as Portsmouth Grammar School. Its facade is, again, a link with the past and one recognised nationally in July 1998 by the government's decision to designate the building as a grade two listed structure to help offer protection from any further development. The appearance is little changed from a 19th century sketch included in Gates's definitive history book of 1927:

'The front portion of Cambridge Barracks shown in the sketch was erected in 1853–4. The back portion is much older. It will be observed that, at the time the barracks were built, the ramparts blocked what is now the entrance to High Street, entrance to which was gained through the Landport Gate opposite Warblington Street.'

Charpentier's 1934 *Guide to Portsmouth and Southsea* added:

'In what has become known as Old Portsmouth, where the largest of the military barracks were situated, it will be observed that an educational establishment has ousted the army of the possession of one big building. This is what were once the officers' quarters at Cambridge Barracks, at the end of High Street. They were acquired in 1928 for an extension to Portsmouth Grammar School.'

The year of the school's purchase was wrong – it was 1926 – but there was no dispute about the fact the building had housed 424 of the 2,321 soldiers based in Portsmouth at the time of the 1891 survey.

The barracks came into being on land previously occupied by the High Street Theatre. The theatre failed in the 1850s, after some 30 years, to be sold to the War Office for £3,500 before the end of 1854.

The building was demolished two years later to make room for an extension to the original Cambridge Barracks. The present barracks building was built on the site occupied by the previous barracks, several adjacent properties and the theatre.

RA's lower ranks lived at Clarence Barracks next door to the Cambridge Barracks home of their officers and the football team. Clarence Barracks was built in 1880 in honour of the Duke of Clarence. This photograph clearly shows the 'architectural exuberance of an extreme sort' which the barracks were said to possess compared to more conventional military premises. The barracks now house the Portsmouth City Museum.

Next door were Clarence Barracks, now Portsmouth's City Museum. They were also on the site of a previous 17th Century barracks and rebuilt in 1824 for the RMLI who stayed there until 1848. The Army took over the building and adopted the name of Clarence Barracks in honour of the Duke of Clarence.

The present building was constructed in 1880 and was described as having 'architectural exuberance of an extreme sort' in contrast to conventional barracks buildings. It became the living quarters of the lower ranks of the RA. Gates noted:

'The barracks were demolished in the eighties of the last century, and a fine range of new buildings erected on the site for the Royal Artillery.'

The fine use the buildings were put to by those men has often been acknowledged during the past century. As the 1906 *Book of Football*, the most comprehensive book of its time about the sport, stated:

'The inhabitants of the great naval port were educated up to association football very gradually. And it's entirely due to the RA football club that a professional team exists. The RA…created a public liking for the game.'

A rare direct personal link back to the days of Royal Artillery can be found through the great grandson of right-back Harms. Bombardier Hugh Roden-Harms, to give the player his full name and title, was one of the regulars of The Gunners' glory years. He was a sports mad Yorkshireman stationed at barracks in Portsmouth.

His great grandson Glen Stanley, an avid Pompey fan, is proud of his relative's role in leading to the creation of the club he now devotedly follows. Glen, of Bishop's Waltham, said:

'My great grandfather sounds like quite a character. From what I understand, he was absolutely obsessed with sport and would think nothing of getting up at 5 am to hit some golf balls. He was known affectionately as HRH or HR bloody H because he played to kill. I think his passion for football has been passed down through the ages and I try to go to as many games as I can.'

Roden-Harms was among the majority of RA players who failed to be taken on by the new Pompey club. The former school physical education teacher had originally chosen football ahead of playing cricket for his county.

But the enthusiasm for sport failed to stop him dying relatively young after being married in Portsmouth in June 1898 at the age of 27.

'My grandmother was known to say that Portsmouth was the death of him and she was probably right,'

said Glen.

Bombardier
Harms

· C H A P T E R   T H I R T Y - E I G H T ·

The FA Files

Two men were responsible for condemning Royal Artillery to history. The pair made up the FA's emergency committee which upheld the initial complaint by Harwich and Parkestion against The Gunners following the sides' Amateur Cup quarter-final in February 1899. J.C. Clegg and C. Crump – both vice-presidents of the FA – were the individuals who ruled that the Artillerymen were professionals. Their verdict, after RA's first appeal to the FA Amateur Cup Committee failed, caused the club to go to the top of the FA.

The Gunners' officials had protested so vigorously and vociferously about their impending demise that the association called the only special general meeting of its members for at least 17 years around the turn of the century. The minutes of that historic occasion, at The Queens Hotel at Birmingham, still survive at the FA's heaquarters in central London.

They occupy a complete page of the minute book and are a mixture of copperplate handwriting – presumably by the secretary of the FA, F.J. Wall – and a printed notice. J.C. Clegg again! – chaired the gathering on April 8, 1899, and Mr Wall read out to the members the notice which had convened the meeting to consider the final appeal by RA against the club's execution as amateurs after the emergency committee had reached the following decision:

'That the payment by the club of the training expenses of the players at Aldeburgh, and of the expenses of the visit of the players to the Crystal Palace, in both respects, constitute an infringement of their status as amateurs, that they must be deemed to be professionals under the rules, and must be registered as such.'

The meeting's outcome, as vital as it was for RA, was noted tersely in the copperplate writing:

'Mr C.D. Crisp of Ryde FC argued the appeal on behalf of the Royal Artillery (Portsmouth) Football Club. Upon a division the appeal was declared to be lost.'

That was the end of RA as a club as far as the Football Association was concerned. But some individual Gunners still featured in its proceedings. Nine of the players who had incurred the FA's wrath a few months previously were re-instated as amateurs in May 1899. Such proceedings were an annual end of season event.

The list which detailed James Brazier, John Coutts, Henry Coleman, John D. Hanna, D. Jardine, J. McNeil, D. Phillips, J. Walsh and F. Woodward was comprised of 88 players. No fewer than 17 were from Lowestoft FC. They and The Gunners found themselves in the company of footballers from such famous clubs as Coventry City, Newton Heath (now Manchester Utd), Thames Ironworks (now West Ham Utd) and Derby County and others whose names were of a more exotic nature.

Soho Villa, White Star Wanderers and Beeston Humber were joined by current semi-professional outfits as Northwich Victoria and Maidenhead in being able to welcome back team members. Besides those re-instated, other players had their cases deferred for a further 12 months.

The affairs of one further Gunner did come before the FA before the team vanished completely as a footballing outfit. The association's emergency committee proceedings of December 31, 1900, to March 29,1901, detailed disciplinary proceedings against Gunner Cook during RA's ill-judged comeback season in the United Services League. The committee heard a report by Sgt M.D.K. Bowden about the player's unspecified alleged misconduct and referred the matter to the Hampshire FA and the Army FA to jointly deal with. Just as bad behaviour by RA's footballers dominated the team's ending in its dealings with the FA, the club's formation was also influenced by the rulings of the association.

Three players who were to have a major influence on RA's affairs were suspended by the association around the period of the formation of The Gunners. The banning of Bomb Hanna, Sergt Morrison and Trumpt Williams – as the FA formally called them – for misconduct was noted in the minutes of the FA council meeting in Chancery Lane, London, on August 9, 1894.

J.C. Clegg began his prominent role n the FA's dealings with Royal Artillery when he chaired the meeting which had a report from the Hampshire FA with details of the suspensions of the Depot RA players for varying periods. Hanna was sidelined until December 31, more than two months after RA's formation, Morrison until September 30 and Williams until September 14. The outbreak of bad behaviour occurred in a match against Cowes. And the FA Council also confirmed the decision of the Hampshire FA about Depot RA's poor conduct in that fixture. The council's previous meeting had discussed the referee's report of the game. It set the scene for a stormy series of fixtures between the clubs.

Next Gunner whose attitude caused the FA to take note was Reilly, of course. So dominant was the Irish keeper in RA's affairs that he was linked to them even in the formal business of the football's ruling body.

So it was that the FA consultative committee, when it met on February 2, 1898, dealt with a report from the southern division emergency committee into Reilly's part in the riot which broke out at the pre-Christmas fixture at Wycombe Wanderers:

'Reilly (Royal Artillery) suspended for 14 days from January 4, 1898.
Wycombe Wanderers FC - ground closed for one week from January 10, 1898.'

Reilly's next dealing with the FA was about a happier matter. Its council meeting of March 29, 1901, approved the staging of a benefit match by Portsmouth FC for their keeper. Five other players were also allowed to enjoy the financial rewards of such a fixture.

The Portsmouth club's formation was similarly formally approved just three years earlier. The second item on the round-up of FA emergency committee proceedings from March 23 to May 12, 1898, read:

PORTSMOUTH FOOTBALL AND ATHLETIC CO LTD
'Memorandum and Articles of Association approved subject to the Football Club being constituted
in accordance with the Rules of the Association, and affiliated to the Hampshire Association.'

The brevity about the birth of a club which was to have a major impact on the life of its home town was typical of how the FA detailed its affairs of the late 19th Century.

Just one word – protest – added to the Amateur Cup quarter-final result between RA and Harwich and Parkeston in the minutes of the Monday, February 27, 1899, meeting of the FA council turned into a death sentence for The Gunners.

Controversy continues

'Last season's football was an eventful one for local followers of the game. The now defunct RA paved the way and educated the populace to take an interest in football. And with their unhappy demise sprang up an entirely new thing for Portsmouth – a properly constituted and well-organised club and Limited Company with plenty of capital, plenty of sportsmen ready to stand by it and thoroughly qualified men to manage it.'   Portsmouth Evening News, May 5, 1900

How ironic those words appear as the centenary season of the professional club unfolds in the most acrimonious of circumstances. Grave doubts existed in the early weeks of 1999 about the future of the Fratton Park outfit.

A hundred years after RA were effectively finished by the FA in a mass of controversy, so the future of football in the city continued to mirror the concern about the continuation of the Artillerymen in 1899 as the past merged into the present.

For the past century has seen another, more unwelcome, legacy of The Gunners passed on to their successors as Portsmouth's footballing flag-bearers – that of making headlines for the wrong reasons.

Early 1999 saw a meeting planned between the FA and one of Portsmouth's MPs into the furore which surrounded affairs at Fratton Park as the future of the club was put into severe doubt. But officials at the FA are no strangers to becoming involved in footballing affairs in the city.

RA were seemingly either protesting to football's ruling body, as occurred after their Amateur Cup final, or were the subject of protests. The most famous of these was their expulsion from the cup in 1899 and, ultimately, from football.

Those fans of the new club who had transferred their allegiances from the USMG to Fratton Park – and the early attendances of 3–7,000 were comparable to RA's – only had a short wait for the bad news to begin.

Even before the *Portsmouth Evening News* had penned its lookback at the professional club's debut season, the supporters had seen their first sign of trouble. It was a matter which has a modern counterpart any fan of Pompey will recognise.

An article in the newspaper in March 1900 described how a Southsea builder was pursuing Portsmouth's directors for money he claimed he was owed for supplying clinker and ash to create the terraces at the new Fratton Park. The matter was a forerunner of the legal action with a building company about an unpaid debt for the KJC Stand (Fratton End) which helped to create the crisis which enveloped the ground as 1998/99 progressed.

As the *Portsmouth Evening News* wrote its praise, the professional club's first season had ended in an £875 loss. That deficit was almost doubled at the end of the following season, 1900/01. The FA soon loomed into view as well to leave ex-Gunners fans with a distinct feeling of *deja vu*.

A special commission was set up in the summer of 1903 by football's ruling body to investigate the transfer of three players from Liverpool. It found against Portsmouth. The club's player-manager, Robert Blyth, was suspended over the issue along with leading player, centre-half Harry Stringfellow.

By 1909/10, Portsmouth were in a severe crisis. Relegation to the Southern League's second division was endured while, off the pitch, losses threatened to escalate out of control. A public appeal brought a good response, while a forthright statement of support from the boardroom helped to stabilise the situation.

But not for long. May 1912 saw the real possibility arise of the end of professional football in Portsmouth after just 14 years. The debts of the football club were excessive and fears were expressed that Fratton Park could become a victim of property developers. They proved groundless. A reformed football club assumed a more business-like footing to enable the playing side to continue.

Another national crisis arose in 1931. The FA began a fresh investigation into the affairs of Portsmouth. The inquiry was again centred on transfer matters. A signing by the club of a player, John Cameron, from a Scottish junior club was contested by Arsenal. The FA ruled neither should take on the player. He went to Tottenham Hotspur instead.

The FA's role in the club's affairs filled the newspapers once more for two of the finest hours experienced by followers of the Fratton Park club. Supporters were so unhappy with the allocation of tickets for the FA Cup final in 1939 they filled the Methodist Central Hall in Fratton with 3,000 protestors.

Eleven years later, and the FA came under attack once more. It took almost two months to announce forward Jimmy Scoular's punishment for being sent off in an England v Scotland international was a 14-day suspension timed to coincide with the last two games of the 1949/50 Football League championship chasing season. Both episodes ended happily for Portsmouth.

The next piece of FA-inspired activity, just a month later, had less of a satisfactory ending. Club chairman Vernon Stokes and director Harry Wain were suspended about irregularities over the return of inside-right James McAlinden from Ireland to Fratton Park just after the Second World War.

It took a 25,000-signature petition from the supporters' club before the FA reinstated the duo in February 1951. The club's £750, the suspension of McAlinden and the censure of manager Jack Tinn continued to stand, however.

And so the story of Portsmouth FC carried on. Financial crises, relegation battles, austerity measures, appeals to the fans. All have played a regular part in the past three decades in the life of a club which has followed in the footsteps of their predecessors at RA in every respect in the past hundred years – controversial, glorious, tumultuous – and always interesting.

· C H A P T E R   F O R T Y ·

Marvellous Marines

High standards set by RA for service football around Portsmouth have been topped once. The honours the second time were gathered by a team based on the opposite side of Portsmouth Harbour. When the 1909/10 season had ended, the Royal Marines Light Infantry side based at Forton Barracks had achieved two unique records. They had become the first side to win both the Amateur and Army cups in a single season and the first to win three Portsmouth Senior League championships in a row. Their triumphs were the biggest footballing success Gosport has ever known. "Sentinel" of the *Football Mail* accorded the team this accolade as 1909/10 came to a close:

> *'To win the Amateur Cup and the Army Cup in one season is a feat any amateur side in the kingdom might justly be proud of. Consistently good, wholehearted and enthusiastic endeavour emerged triumphant again and again.'*

The crowds who turned out to acknowledge the achievements of RMLI –The Lilywhites – can safely be given the status as Gosport's largest sports-related gathering.

Some 10,000 people – estimated as half the town's population at the time – poured into the barracks' square after The Lilywhites had gone one better than RA and become Amateur Cup holders on April 18.

The team returned just before 6 pm that evening to be greeted by 2–3,000 people at the Portsmouth Town Station. The reception was far more organised than any held by RA. And it was far more comprehensively reported following the *Football Mail*'s development into a fully-fledged newspaper.

Sgt Gowney, The Lilywhites' secretary and manager, and the team's captain, Hirst, who held the cup decked in white ribbons, waved delightedly in response to the cheers. But the duo promptly boarded a decorated brake and drove away to the Gosport ferry to foil the hopes of the supporters of getting a closer look at the coveted trophy. Their fellow Marines and the police had to be brought in to control the crowd which greeted the team in Gosport. The uniformed presence managed to clear a space around the fountain where only the second civic reception in the town's history took place.

District council chairman Mr T.M. McCully reminded everyone present the previous occasion followed the defeat by the Marines of the Egyptians by showing pluck and determination. Sgt Gowney briefly responded before the RMLI band led the way for the victory parade through the High Street, North Cross Street, North Street, Clarence Road and Forton Road to the masses crowded inside the barracks.

Hirst briefly broke away from the celebrations to tell a reporter the Amateur Cup final opponents South Bank, from North East England, were not the best team The Lilywhites had faced 'but they were the best cup fighters'. But he said the Marines won because of one factor: 'We kept our heads and they seemed to get excited'.

RMLI had overcome the toughest opposition, it was reckoned, to reach the final at Bishop Auckland before 10,000 spectators. They had played four away games in the competition proper in defeating Worthing (4–0), Bournemouth (3–1), Bromley (2–1) and Custom House (2–1) in successive rounds before Tufnell Park were despatched 4–0 at Fratton Park. Opponents in a further four qualifying rounds had also been overcome.

South Bank, meanwhile, had earned themselves a tough reputation when they knocked out the renowned Clapton in the semi-finals. It was of no use against The Lilywhites. The Gosport side went 2–0 up within 30 minutes in spite of having virtually no support among the crowd because of the lengthy journey required from the south coast.

RMLI's first goal was netted by right-winger Jack with a 14th minute header after a perfect centre from Exford. Holness, the centre-forward, added to the lead on 30 minutes after some nice exchanges between his team-mates. It became the turn of the Marines' defence to come to the fore as South Bank attacked continuously.

They stood firm before half-time but Biggs pulled a goal back for South Bank four minutes after the restart. The pressure was on the RMLI as their opponents pressed for the equalizer. One mistake by the Marines' defence on a pitch turned into a footballers' greasy nightmare by constant rain would have been all it needed for the northerners to draw level.

The Marines' team in the final: Turner, Wilkinson, Hirst (Cpt), Revill, Yates, Wiseman, Exford, White, Holness, Smith, Jack was missing one regular. Left-winger Spackman was in Haslar Hospital, Gosport, because of a knee injury sustained in the Army Cup final two weeks previously.

The earlier final had also seen a 10,000-strong crowd waiting – on that occasion at Gosport railway station – to see the cup heroes return at 9.10 pm on Easter Monday, the traditional Army Cup final day. Hirst and Yates were carried shoulder high by their fellow players and other Marines through the throng. Hirst proudly displayed the cup. Yates held on to the replica trophy which was kept by the winning side.

That afternoon had seen Smith score from a Jack pass and Jack convert a centre from Exford to earn the RMLI a 2–0 victory against the 2nd Royal Irish Fusiliers. The crowd at the Aldershot venue numbered 18,000. *The Portsmouth Evening News* and the *Football Mail* were ecstatic about the success achieved by a side reduced to ten men by Spackman's injury.

The setback, shortly after the Marines had gone a goal up just before half-time, seemed to spur the side on even though a further two players were limping passengers as the game ended.

The newspapers reported:

> *'The RMLI (Forton) reached the height of their ambitions when they received the Army Cup from the Prince of Wales at Aldershot after beating the Irish Fusiliers. In all military sport there is no greater honour than the winning of the Army Football Cup under association rules and the magnificent performance of the RMLI… has brought an additional and well-merited honour to that redoubtable corps. The team travelled to Aldershot with a certain amount of confidence that they would win. They realised their opponents were a fairly good side. At the start, it seemed the Fusiliers would score the first goal and Wilkinson was playing weakly but this was only temporary and, after Smith scored, the Marines played a winning game. They kept the ball on the swing whereas their opponents adopted close play. Brilliant forward play secured for the Marines their victory. Their defence also deserves credit.'*

RMLI's team was: Turner, Wilkinson, Hirst, Revall, Yates, Wiseman, Exford, Smith, Holness, Jack, Spackman. It had been March 1904 since a team based in the Portsmouth area had reached the Army Cup final. The RMA had then defeated the Depot Battalion to clinch the trophy. But The Lilywhites' stood supreme above that achievement for the scale of their successes.

On April 28, 1910, they defeated Gosport United 5–1 at home to clinch the unprecedented third Portsmouth League title in a row. Their league record was worthy of the impressive feat:

P19 W15 D3 L1 F57 A12 Pts 33

The honours list was completed by the United Services League division two championship won by the Marines' reserves. *The Portsmouth Evening News* was quick to point out the magnitude of the performance of RMLI. Winning the league was the 'crowning glory of a really remarkable period of prosperity':

> *'Their success during the last three years has been quite phenomenal. They have won practically every competition for which they are eligible.'*

The team passed into history without the lasting impact of RA, though *Football Mail* readers anxious to discover how Pompey's league championship bid in February 1949 was faring had a brief reminder of the Lilywhites' prowess.

The newspaper's columnist, "Ranger", told how he had met Charles Wilkinson, of the RMLI, during his visit to Sheffield Utd to watch Pompey play.

He reminded them that, 40 years previously, Wilkinson had been amassing an impressive array of honours – three times successive Portsmouth League champion, and winner of the Portsmouth Senior Cup, Amateur Cup, Army Cup and US Charity Cup as well as being an army international.

FOOTBALL / Outstanding team of marines scooped amateur trophy in 1910

Gosport's FA Cup glory

■ Team were given a hero's welcome when they crossed harbour from Portsmouth.

The 75 years that the Royal Marine Light Infantry were housed in Gosport was a happy period for the town.

Many marines married local girls and a strong family community grew up around the barracks at Forton.

And yet it was only by chance that they came to the town, for before 1848 they were a firm fixture in Portsmouth, quartered at the Cambridge Barracks, Southsea.

However, their presence was not good for the governor's ego for he took great delight in presenting grand military displays and the RMLI were not colourful or exciting enough.

So governor Lord Frederick Fitzclarence had them transferred out of sight at Forton.

Pompey's loss was Gosport's gain, for they contributed greatly to the prosperity of the town and its everyday life.

One day in 1910, the RMLI at Forton put Gosport well and truly on the map. It was a day that they would have engraved in their memory cells for years to come.

The RMLI always fielded good football teams in the local leagues, but their team of 1910 was exceptional, not only locally but nationally.

Their first success took place

PORTSMOUTH DIVISION. 1909-10

The RMLI football team of 1910, who won the Army Cup and the FA Amateur Cup

How The News *in 1998 reported RMLI's triumphs.*

Statistics

Abbreviations used in the following tables

AmC .... Amateur Cup
ArC .... Army Cup
ArtyC .... Artillery Cup
EC .... English Cup
HSC .... Hampshire Senior Cup
HSL .... Hampshire Senior League
PSC/PDC .... Portsmouth Senior Cup/Portsmouth District Cup
RAC .... Royal Artillery Cup
SDRA .... Southern District Royal Artillery
SL .... Southern League
USL .... United Services League
USMG .... United Services Men's Ground
USOG .... United Services Officers' Ground

Numbers next to a player's position indicate goals scored

Anyone who expects Victorian newspapers to include the full range of statistics usually found in their late 20th Century counterparts will quickly realise their mistake. Statistics were less highly rated in football's early years. Their details varied greatly from day to day and even edition to edition among the six daily versions of the *Portsmouth Evening News*. The facts used in this section have usually been drawn from the *Portsmouth Evening News*, with additions from the *Southern Daily Mail* and the *Portsmouth Times*. The exception is the 1900/01 season. This has been compiled principally from the *Southern Daily Mail* and the *Portsmouth Times*. Using these newspapers, and others from around the country, has enabled me to piece together the most detailed facts about RA's birth and death known to date. But one game shows the difficulties in trying to work out the correct information.

RA played 15th Co SDRA in November 1894. The first game was abandoned after 20 minutes and was given as an Artillery Cup first round tie. The replay was said to be in the Hampshire Senior Cup. Similar instances abounded throughout RA's early history. Different spellings of a player's name and even inconsistent results were reported. I have listed the variations where I thought it was appropriate. But, on occasions, it has been impossible to decide what the journalist saw as he stood at ground level among thousands of spectators at a wet and windy US Men's Ground in mid-winter. These statistics can, therefore, only be so complete and so accurate. But the history those journalists recorded is well worth re-telling a hundred years later.

KEVIN SMITH

1893 - 1894 15th Co RA and Depot RA

Date	Teams	Competition	Venue	Attendance	W/L/D	Result	Duff/Duffy/Duffey/Gnr	Reilly/Riley Gnr	Logan/Hogan Gnr	Traynor	Williams Trumpeter	Patterson Gnr	Morrison Cpl	Maxwell Gnr	Hanna Bbr	Sampson/Simpson/Samson Gnr	Scott Gnr	Moss	Roddy	Macauley	Monaghan	Pringle	Nelson	Connelly	Harms Bbr
13.01	15th Co SDRA v RMA		Eastney		W	5-1																			
17.01	Depot RA v Connaught Rangers	PDC R2	USMG		W	5-1	1	2	3^{1}	4	5	6	7	8^{1}	9^{2}	10^{1}	11								
22.01	15th Co SDRA v Woolwich Arsenal Res		a		L	2-5																			
23.01	Depot RA v Portsmouth Garrison		a		W	2-1			2		10^{1}		8^{1}	7			1	3	4	5	6	9	11		
29.01	15th Co SDRA v St Mary's (Soton)		a	Large concourse of people	W	3-1																			
10.02	Depot RA (G'pt) v St Mary's (Soton)		USMG	Large crowd	D	0-0	4	1	3		5	6	7	8	9	10	11								2
14.02	15th Co SDRA v Depot RA (Rowner)	RAC	USMG	2,000	W	2-1	6	1	3		5		8	9^{1}	4	10	11	Depot RA team						7	2
17.02	Depot SDRA v St Mary's (Soton)	PDC s-f	USMG		L	1-3	4	1	3		5	6	8	7^{1}	9	11	10								2
20.02	RA (G'pt) v 1st Royal Scots Fusiliers	ArC R5	County Ground, Leyton		W	3-1								p^{1}	p^{1}	p^{1}									
21.03	15th Co SDRA v Connaught Rangers		Fareham Rec Grd		W	4-0																			
21.03	Depot RA v S Wales Borderers		USMG		W	4-0								p^{1}	p^{3}										
end March	2nd Bt Gordon Highlanders	ArC s-f	Derby		W	4-1																			
29.03	15th Co (F'ham) v 4th Co Golden Hill (IoW)	RAC f	USMG	Large mass of spectators	W	4-0																			
31.03	15th Co SDRA (F'ham) v Royal Engineers (Aldershot)	Charity cup	County Ground, Soton		W	5-0																			
04.04	RA (G'pt) v 2nd Black Watch	ArC f	Aldershot	15,000	L	2-7	4	1	3		5	6	11	10^{1}	9^{1}	8	7								2
09.04	15th Co v Cowes		a		W	2-1																			
18.04	15th Co SDRA v Romsey	Benefit match	a	Large attendance	W	3-0																			
23.04	15th Co SDRA v St Mary's (Soton)	Charity cup	City Grd, Soton	Large attendance	L	1-5																			

Notes: 17.01 Connaught Rangers - Logan named as Hogan in scorers

14.02 15th Co team - Knight Moorhouse McKie Harper Brownlie Haxton Jackman (1) Nicholls Cook Hailin McDonald (1)

29.03 15th Co team - Knight Moorhouse McKie Harper Brownlie Haxton Jackson (1) Leonard Cook (1) McDonald Nicholls (2)

1894 -1895

Date	Teams	Competition	Venue	Attendance	W/L/D	Result	Reilly/Riley Gnr	Phillips Gnr	Williams/Williams E	Roberts Sgt	Patterson Gnr	Hill Gnr	Robertson	Howe	Williams Sgt	Samson/Sampson	Pugh	Scott	Leonard	Doyle	Brogue	Arnold	Kinman/Kingsman Gnr	Walsh Cpl	Newey	Hanna/Hannah Bbr	Phinn/Finn	Moss	Jardine Gnr	Hogg Gnr	Harris/Harmes Bbr	Fletcher Gnr	Maxwell Gnr	Allen Bbr	Moore	Lavery
06.10	Portsmouth Grammar School		h		W	2-0	1	2	3	4	5	6¹	7	8	9¹	10	11																			p¹
23.10	RMA	ArC1	h		W	1-0	1	3	2		5	6				10¹		11	9	8	7	4															(plus unknown scorer)
02.11	Scottish Cameronians		h		D	2-2			p¹																											(plus unknown scorer)
03.11	United Victorias		h		W	8-1	1	2	3	6	4²	5			9³	7³		8		10																(only ten men listed in line-up)
10.11	15th Co SDRA (F'ham)	ArtyC1	a		D	0-0																	Abandoned - 20 minutes												
17.11	Portsmouth Grammar School	PSC1	a		W	1-0																													
24.11	15th Co SDRA (F'ham)	HSC	a		L	0-3																	Score also given as 1-3 - no scorer listed												
28.11	RMA		h		W	3-0																													
08.12	Havant		a		W	3-1																													
15.12	Lancaster (King's Own) Rgt	PSC2	h	1,500	L	0-4	1	3	2		6	5			8	11													10		9				4	
28.12	Portsmouth Wanderers		h		W	4-1														p¹							p¹				p¹					
29.12	Bournemouth		a		W	3-2	p	p	p¹				p¹																							
05.01	Army Service Corps		a		W	7-0				p¹																p²	p¹	p²								
12.01	Southsea Rovers		h		D	1-1																	No result - limited to 60 minutes												
16.01	Lancaster (King's Own) Rgt		h	large number of spectators	W	5-0																													
05.02	King's Royal Rifles	ArC3	h	large number of spectators	W	5-0	1	2	7		6	5			7¹	11¹		4					3			9¹	8¹		10¹							p¹
16.02	Cowes		a		L	1-2																													
26.02	15th Co SDRA (F'ham)	ArCR4	h	1,500	W	2-0	1	3	7		4							10					2			9¹			11		5	8¹			6	
14.03	W Kent Rgt	ArC5	a		W	3-0	1								9	11							5								5		7			
23.03	Southsea Rovers		a		W	2-0	1	3	7		4					11							6			9¹			10¹	3	2				8	
03.04	Royal Scots Fusiliers	ArC s-f	Guildford	good attendance	W	1-0	1	2	8		5					11							6 / 10			9¹			11	4	2		7			
15.04	2nd Black Watch	ArC final	Aldershot	12,000	W	2-0					4				9								6			8²			7	5	3		11 10			

1895 - 1896

Date	Teams	Competition	Venue	Attendance	W/L/D	Result	Notes / Scorers
07.09	New Brompton		a	3,000	L	0-2	no scorers given
14.09	Luton Town		a	close to 5,000	L	1-6	
23.09	London Welsh		a	about 1,000	D	0-0	
28.09	Freemantle		a		W	4-1	
01.10	RMA		a		W	2-0	
14.10	Dublin Fusiliers		h		W	6-0	
18.10	Reading		a		L	0-3	
27.10	Tottenham Hotspur		a		W	2-1	scorer possibly Meggs
29.10	Dublin Fusiliers	ArC1	h		W	5-0	
02.11	Clifton	AmC2q	a	about 2,000	W	10-0	
09.11	Bristol South End	EC2	a		W	0-0	
16.11	Bristol St Georges					Game scratched by Bristol St Georges	
26.11	15th Co RA (Gosport)	ArC2	h	large crowd	W	3-1	
30.11	15th Co RA (Fareham)	HSC2	a		W	5-1aet 1-1 90m	
02.12	Eastbourne		a		L	0-2	
16.12	Old Weymouthians	AmC4q	h	about 2,000	W	5-1	
28.12	Southampton		a		L	2-6	
04.01	Southsea Rovers	PSC2	a		W	6-0	no scorers given
16.01	Weymouth Athletic		a		D	0-0	
17.01	Cowes		a		W	3-2	
18.01	Portsmouth Wanderers		h			3-0	RA at full strength
01.02	3rd Grenadier Guards	AmC1	h	upwards 4,000	D	1-1	
08.02	3rd Grenadier Guards	AmC1r	h	some 5,000	D	2-2 aet 1-1 90m	
11.02	Royal Irish Rifles	ArC3	a	2,000	D	0-0 aet 0-0 90m	
13.02	3rd Grenadier Guards	AmC1/2	a	300	W	1-0	
15.02	Middlesborough	AmC2	a		W	2-1	
19.02	Royal Irish Rifles	Arc3r	h	over 3,000	W	3-1	
22.02	RMLI	PSCs-f			D	1-1	
26.02	Freemantle	HSCs-f	City Gd, Soton	numerous midweek gate	W	1-0	plus unknown scorer
29.02	Maidenhead	AmC3	a	good gate	W	5-0	plus unknown scorers
04.03	South Lancashire Rgt	ArC5	a	900	W	5-2 aet 2-2 90m	
07.03	St Mary's Reserves	HSCf	h		W	3-0	no scorers given
10.03	RMLI	PSC s-f r	h	about 1,000	W	5-0	
17.03	Royal Scots (Chatham)	ArC s-f	Tufnell Park	some 2,000	L	1-2	
21.03	Shrewsbury	AmC f	Reading	about 1,500	W	2-0	
28.03	Bishop Auckland	AmC f	Leicester Fosse	large crowd	W	0-1	
11.04	15th Co RA	PSC f		3,000	L	0-1	

The players (column headers, rotated) were: Reilly/Ryley Gnr, Hamms/Arms Bdr, Phillips Gnr, Harper Gnr, Hill Gnr, Patterson/Batterson Gnr, Meggs/Maggs Gnr/Br/Bdr, Maxwell Gnr, Hannah/Hannah Bdr, Williams Sgt, Jardine Gnr, McNeill/McNeill Gnr, Cook/Cooke Gnr, Little, Welsh/Walsh Cpl, Hannes, Kinman Gnr, Hoff/Hogg Gnr, Hooper, Fletcher Gnr, Hamson, McDonald Gnr, Haxton Gnr, Walton, Brazier Gnr, Stewart Gnr, Jackson, Tyre.

Notes:

10.02 Dublin Fusiliers v RA scratched

19.02 Attendance given as several thousands in the *Southern Daily Mail*. Army Cup 4 no details of game

11.04 Game described as the Portsmouth Town Cup final.

11.04 RA's opponents, Portsmouth Town FC, scratched in the PSC1

02.10 Score given as 11-0 in the *Portsmouth Evening News* but only ten goal scorers given

29.10 Given as HSC1 in *Hampshire Telegraph*

Date	Teams	Competition	Venue	Attendance	W/L/D	Result	Fletcher Gnr	Harms Cpl	Reilly Gnr	Hill Gnr	Philips Gnr	Hanna Cpl	Meggs/Maggs Bbr	Walsh/Welsh Cpl	Cook Gnr	Brazier	Jardine Gnr	McKenzie Gnr	Hogg/Hoggs Gnr	Kinman Gnr	Haxton	Tyre Gnr	Jones	Moore	Williams Sgt	Doyle	Whittle	Patterson Gnr	Coleman Sgt	Coatts	Dodd	McCabe Gnr	Walton
26.09	Andover	HSL	h	500	W	8-0	1	2	3	4	5	6[1]	7	8[4]	9[2]	10[1]	11																
03.10	Eastleigh	HSL	h	nearly 3,000	W	3-0		2	1	5	3	9	7	8[1]	11[2]		10	4	6														
10.10	Eastleigh	EC prem 1	h	ropes well lined	W	2-1 aet 1-1 90m		2	1	5	3	9[1]	7[1]	8		11	10	4		6						game stopped, fading light								
14.10	Eastleigh	EC prem 1	h	3,000	W	7-1		2	1	6	3	9[1]	8[2]	7			10[1]	4				5	11[3]										
17.10	Bournemouth	HSL	a		W	4-0		2	1	6	3	9	7[1]	8			11[2]	5		4			10[1]										
24.10	Oxford Cygnets	EC prem 2	a		W	3-1 aet 1-1 90m		2	1	6	3	10[1]	7[1]	8	9		11	4			5				plus unknown scorer								
29.10	Royal Sussex Rgt	ArC1	h	fairly large crowd	W	3-1		2	1	6	3	5[2]	7	8	9[1]		11	4					10										
31.10	HMS Vernon	PSC prem	h		W	9-0	1	2		5									9		4		11[5]	3	6	7	8[1]	10						
14.11	Dublin Fusiliers	PSC 1	h	considerable crowd	W	15-0		2[1]	1	6	3	10[5]	7[3]	8[3]	9[2]		11[1]	5		4														
28.11	East Lancashire Rgt	HSC2	h	nearly 5,000	W	1-0		2	1	5	3	10	7	8	9		11			4			own goal - Everett					6					
05.12	Ryde	HSL	h	fairly good crowd	W	7-0		3	1	5[1]	3	2	11[1]	7[1]	8[1]	9[1]	10[1]			4									6[1]					
12.12	Swindon T	EC prem 3	a	small attendance	L	1-4		2	1	5	3	10	8[1]	7	9		11			4									6					
02.01	Cowes	HSL	h	about 3,000	D	2-2		2	1			5	7	8[1]	9		11[1]	4		3			10						6					
09.01	Ryde	HSL	a		W	5-1		2	1			5[1]	7[1]	8	9		11[1]						10	plus unknown scorer			6	3	4				
13.01	Freemantle	HSL	a		D	1-1		2	1		3	5	7	8[1]	9		11	4										6	10				
03.02	Army Service Corps	PSC s-f			W	15-0		2	1	6[1]	3	5[2]	7[3]	8[2]	11					4[1]			10		own goal - Bick			9[5]					
06.02	Cowes	HSC s-f	Southampton	fair	L	0-1		2	1	6	3	5	7	8	10					4			11					9					
10.02	Old Etonians	AmC1	a	small crowd	W	3-2		2	1	5	3	4	9	8	10		2						11					6	7[1]				
13.02	Casuals	AmC2	a		L	2-3		2	1		3[1]	10		8	9		11			4[1]	5							6	7				
17.02	Gosport RA	ArC2	h		W	3-0		2[1]	1	6	3	10		8	9[1]		11	5		4									7[1]				
20.02	St Mary's Reserves	HSL	h	very large crowd	W	4-0		2	1	6[2]	3	10[1]	7	8	9		11[1]			4	5												
28.02	King's Own Lancs Rgt	ArC3	a	2,000	W	6-1		2	1	6	3	5[2]	8	7	9[1]		11[1]			4[1]			plus unknown scorer					10				
06.03	Andover	HSL	a	capital attendance	W	6-0		2	1	6	3[1]	10	7	8[1]	9[2]		11[1]	5		4													
17.03	2nd East Lancs Rgt	ArC4	a	7,000	W	1-0		2	1	6	3	5	11[1]	10	9		7			4								8					
20.03	Southsea Rovers	PSC f	USMG	good	W	5-0		2	1	4	3	5[1]	7[1]	8	9		11[3]			6								10					
24.03	St Mary's Reserves	HSL	a		W	3-0						p[1]			p[2]																		
27.03	Bournemouth	HSL	h	fair	W	6-0		2	1	6	3	10[1]	7[1]	8	9[2]		11[1]			4	5											1[1]	
03.04	Freemantle	HSL	h		W	2-0		2	1	4	3		7[1]	8	9[1]		11			6	5												10
08.04	3rd Grenadier Guards	ArC s-f	County Grd, Southampton		D	1-1 aet 1-1 90m		2	1	6	3	5	7	8	9		11			4			plus unnamed scorer					10				
14.04	3rd Grenadier Guards	ArC s-f r	Guildford		W	2-1		2	1	6	3	5	7[1]	8	9		11			4			plus unnamed scorer					10				
19.04	Lancashire Fusiliers	ArC f	Aldershot	about 15,000	W	1-0		2	1	6	3	5	7	8	9		11[1]			4								10				
24.04	Cowes	HSL	a	2,300	L	0-1		2	1	4	3		7	8	10		11			6	5							9				
28.04	Eastleigh	HSL	h	good	D	3-3		2	1	6	3		7	8[1]	10		11			4	5		plus unnamed scorer					9[1]				

Notes: PSC2 RMLI scratched

  EC prem 3 Eastville Rovers scratched

  03.10 Crowd in *Portsmouth Times* as 3,000, receipts £39

  10.02 Jardine in match reports as scoring twice but not listed in line-up

  07.11 HSC1 Ryde scratched. Played instead as friendly. Ryde 2 RA 3 'considerable interest' Reilly, Harms, Jones, Kinman, McKenzie, Hill, Meggs, Walsh, Tyre, Doyle, Jardine. No scorers given

  17.03 attendance given in *Portsmouth Evening News* as over 3,000

  28.04 game played at Governor's Green. Originally scheduled for December 19 at Eastleigh

  07.01 Sandown 5 RA 0 - 'exceptional gate' listed in *Portsmouth Evening News*, no other details

  27.03 McCabe in match reports as scoring but not listed in line-up

Date	Teams	Competition	Venue	Attendance	W/L/D	Result
04.09	Eastleigh	HSL	a		L	1-5
11.09	St Mary's Reserves	HSL	h	1,500-2,000	W	2-0
18.09	Freemantle	HSL	a	small	D	1-1
25.09	Ryde	HSL	a		L	0-1
02.10	Warmley	SL2	a		L	0-2
09.10	Uxbridge	SL2	a	500-600	W	1-0
13.10	Royal Sussex Rgt	ArC1	h	very good crowd	W	4-1
16.10	Old St Stephen's	SL2	a	2,000	W	4-1
23.10	West Herts	SL2	a	fairly large attendance	D	2-2
30.10	Cowes	EC3q	a	some 2,000	D	1-1
04.11	Cowes	EC3q r	h	unusually large crowd	D	2-2 aet / 2-2,9&m
06.11	Andover	HSL	h	ropes well-lined	W	3-1
08.11	Cowes	EC3q 2r	a	about 2,000	L	0-1
10.11	2nd Bt Scottish Rifles	ArC2	h	another big crowd	W	4-0
13.11	Cowes	HSL	a	about 1,000	W	1-0
17.11	1st Bt Worcs Rgt	ArC3	a		W	3-1
27.11	Dartford	SL2	h	large crowd of onlookers	W	2-0
04.12	Royal Engineers' Training Battalion (Chatham)	SL2	h	large crowd	W	4-1
09.12	Southall	SL2	a	small attendance	W	3-2
11.12	Maidenhead	SL2	h	usual large crowd	W	9-0
18.12	Maidenhead	SL2	a	goodly gathering	W	5-0
20.12	Wycombe Wanderers	SL2	a	good crowd	W	3-1
15.01	Chetham	SL2	h	large crowd	W	8-1
22.01	Warmley	SL2	h	no less than 7,000	W	2-1
29.01	St Albans	SL2	a		W	2-0
05.02	West Herts	SL2	h	large crowd assembled	W	2-0
12.02	1st Royal Scots Fusiliers	ArC4	a	1,500	W	5-1
12.02	RETB (Chatham)	SL2	a	nearly 1,000	W	5-1
19.02	Uxbridge	SL2	h	usual large crowd	W	5-0
26.02	Dartford	SL2	a		W	2-1
02.03	Ryde	HSL	h	large number	D	1-1
05.03	Freemantle	HSL	h	2,000-odd	W	6-0
09.03	Wycombe Wanderers	SL2	h		W	3-1
12.03	Eastleigh	HSL	h	unusually large crowd	W	5-1
14.03	Chesham	SL2	a	good crowd	W	3-1
19.03	Andover	HSL	a	capital attendance	W	2-1
24.03	2nd North Staffs Rgt	ArC s-f	Stoke	moderate attendance	W	3-0
26.03	St Albans	SL2	h		W	4-1
30.03	Southall	SL2	h		W	2-1
02.04	St Mary's Reserves	HSL	a	200	L	2-3
04.04	Old St Stephen's	SL2	h		L	1-5
11.04	2nd Gordon Highlanders	ArCf	Aldershot	17,000	W	6-0
16.04	Cowes	HSL	h	large crowd	D	1-1
19.04	Wolverton L and NW Railway	SL test match	h		D	3-3
23.04	Wolverton L and NW Railway	SL test match	a	100	W	1-0
27.04	Northfleet	SL test match	a		W	3-1
30.04	Northfleet	SL test match	h		W	1-0

Player columns (as column headings): Tyre, Walton, McBirnie, Brown, Griffiths, Gerrard/Jerard, Paley, Brazier, Woodward, Meggs Bbr, Blount Lt, Phillips Gnr, Prebend, Patterson Gnr, Jardine Gnr, Lewis, Ward, Turner Gnr, Coutts, McCabe Gnr, MacKenzie Gnr, Hill Gnr, Maxwell Gnr, Phinn, McNeill/McNeil Gnr, Coleman/Colman Sgt, Hanna Sgt, Booth, Walsh Cpl, Kinman/Kingman Gnr, Harris Cpl, Haxton, Reilly Gnr

Notes: 13.11 PSC1 a 15th Co RA scratched
18.12 attendance in Southern Daily Mail as 'small'
12.02 RA opener 'impossible to see scorer'
12.02 RA third goal - Patterson free-kick shaved Meggs's shoulder on way in
19.03 plus own goal - Beale

Date	Teams	Competition	Venue	Attendance	W/L/D	Result	Reilly Gnr	Turner Gnr	Woodard	Clarke Lt	Phillips Gnr	Hanna Sgt	Coleman Sgt	Walsh Cpl	Phinn	Brazier	Jardine Gnr	Hill Gnr	Meggs Bbr	Patterson Gnr	McNeil Gnr	Coutts	Queenan	Harris Cpl	Leach	Whitehouse	Sutherland	Smith	Harrison	Taylor	Woods	McBirnie/MacBirnie	Dodds	McGibbon	Willacks/Willocks	Field	Bowyer
03.09	Swindon T	SL1	a	4,000	L	2-3	1	2	3	4	5^1	6	7	8	9	10^1	11																					
21.09	Reading	SL1	h	2,000	D	1-1	1	2	3	4		6	7	8	9	10	11	5	7	6																	
24.09	Brighton Utd	SL1	a	good crowd	L	0-8	1	2	3	4		6	7	8	9	10	11	5	7	6																	
01.10	Weymouth	EC1q	h	about 2,000	W	5-0	1	2	3	4		4	8	8^1	9	10	11	5	7^2	6	9																
05.10	Millwall Ath	SL1	h	big crowd	L	1-2	1	2	3	4	3	4	8	11	10		11	5	7^1	6																	
08.10	Southampton	SL1	a		L	1-4	1	2	3									5	7	6																	
15.10	Cowes	EC2q	h	large crowd	D	1-1	1	2	3		3	4	8	9	9^1	10		5	7	6	4																
20.10	Cowes	EC2q r	a	1,500	L	0-3	p	2																													
22.10	Brighton Utd	SL1	h	big crowd	W	2-0	1	2	3		3	4^1	7	8	9	10^1	11	5	9	6	8																
26.10	1st Bt Rifle Brigade	ArC1	a	2,000	W	5-1	1	2	3		3	4^2	7^1	9^2	10		11	5	9	6	8																
29.10	Chatham	SL1	a	2,000	L	0-5	1	2	3		3	4	7	9			11	5	9	6	8																
05.11	Warmley	SL1	h	quite 3,000	D	2-2	1	2	3		3	9^3	7	8			11	5	9	6	4																
09.11	1st Bt East Lancashire Rgt	ArC2	h		W	7-2	1	2		4	3	9^1	7	9	8	10^1	11^1	5		6																	
12.11	Gravesend Utd	SL1	h	over 2,000	D	1-1	1	2			3	4	7	9	8	10	11	5		6	4																
26.11	Tottenham Hotspur	SL1	a	huge crowd	L	2-3	1	2			3	4	7	8	8^1	10	11	5		6	9^1																
03.12	New Brompton	SL1	h	1,500	L	1-2	p	2			3	p^3	7	8	8^1	p^1		5		6	9																
07.12	1st Bt Royal Welsh Fusiliers	ArC3	a	3,000	W	8-1	p	2			3	5	7	8	8^1			p^1		6	9	4^1	10														
17.12	Southampton	SL1	h		D	1-1	1	2			3	5^1	7	8	8^1	10	11	p^1		6	9	4															
31.12	Sheppey Utd	SL1	h	very fair crowd but not so many thousands as usual	W	1-0	1	2			3	8	7	8			11	5		6	9	4															
07.01	Tottenham Hotspur	SL1	a	4,000	L	0-1	1	2			3	9	7	8		10	11	5		6	9	4															
09.01	Millwall Ath	SL1	h	2,000	L	0-6	1	2			3	9	7	8		10	11	5		6	9	4															
14.01	New Brompton	SL1	a	5,000	L	0-2	1	2			3	9	7	8		10	11	5		6	9	4															
21.01	Warmley	SL1	a	about 200	W	2-1	p	2		4	3	9^2	7	8		10^1	11	5		6	9	4															
28.01	Kirkley	AmC1	h		W	4-0	1	2			3	9^1	7	8		10	11	5		6	$8^=$	4															
04.02	Chatham	AmC2	h	about 4,000	D	1-1	1	2			3	9	7	8		10	11	5		6	9	4															
11.02	Marlow	AmC2	h	fair crowd	W	2-0	1	2			3	9^1	7^1	8		10	11	5		6^1	9	4															
25.02	Harwich & Parkeston	AmC3	a	4-5,000	W	3-1	1	2			3	9	7	8		10^1	11	5		6	9	4^1															
04.03	Gravesend Utd	SL1	h		L	0-3	1	2			3	9	7	8		10	11	5		6	9	4															
11.03	Swindon T	SL1	h	large crowd	W	1-0	1	2			3	9	7	8	9	10	11	5		6	9	4															
16.03	1st South Lancashire Rgt	ArC s-f	Aston Lower Ground	2,000	L	1-3 aet / 1-1 90m	1	2			3	9^1	7	8	9	10^1	11	5		6	9	4															
18.03	Bristol C	SL1	h	good attendance even larger than usual	L	0-3	1	2			3	9	7	8	10	10	11	5		6^1	9	4															
25.03	Sheppey Utd	SL1	a	1,000 or more	W	1-0	1	2			3	9^1	7	8	10	10^1	11	5		6	9	4															
31.03	Bedminster	SL1	a	fair gate	W	1-0	p	p		3	p			8	9	10	p^1	5		6	9	4											1				
08.04	Bedminster	SL1	h	large crowd	L	0-2	1	2		3		8^1	7	8		10	11	5		6	9	4			1	2	4	5	6	7	8	10	11					
12.04	Bristol C	SL1	a	2,000	L	1-6	1	2		3				8		10	11	5		6	9	4			2	4	5	6	7	8	10	11	8	7			
22.04	Reading	SL1	a	small attendance	L	0-5	1	2						8	9	10	11	5		6	9	4			1	2	5	6	7	8	10	4	8	9	11	1	
29.04	Cowes	SL test match	Southampton	poor attendance	L	1-4	1	2				8^1		8	9	10	11	5		6	9	4			1^2	2	6	7	8	10	4	8	7	9	11		4

Notes:

11.02 RA called The Blossoms
14.01 attendance in *Southern Daily Mail* 'quite 3,000'
17.01 attendance in *Southern Daily Mail* 6,000
17.12 attendance in *Southern Daily Mail* 'quite 3,000' / in *Portsmouth Times* 'fully 8,000'
26.10 Scorers given in *Portsmouth Times* as Hanna 3, Walsh 2
28.01 Walsh and McNeil both named as scorers

plus unnamed scorer
plus unnamed scorers

1900-1901

Column group header: Simpson, Moss, Haxton/Huxton, Sutherland, Haynun/Hayhurst — **plus unnamed scorers**

Date	Teams	Competition	Venue	Attendance	W/L/D	Result	Harms Cpl	Phillips Gnr	Harper Gnr	Coleman Sgt	Cook/Cooke Gnr	Jardine Gnr	Walsh/Watch Cpl	Benson	Dodds	Parmer/Palmer	McNeil Gnr	Simpson	Moss	Haxton/Huxton	Sutherland	Haynun/Hayhurst	Harrison	Hendry	Davey	MacMillan	Savage	Hill Gnr
24.10	RA Hilsea	USL	a		W	6-1	p		p	p	p³	p	p															
27.10	HMS Excellent	USL	h		L	2-4								p¹	p¹													
31.10	Naval Depot	USL	h	large crowd	W	1-0	p			own goal - Simpson	p					p			p									
03.11	Ryde	HSC1	a		L	1-3																						
07.11	20th Co RA	USL	h		W	6-0	p¹				p³						p²											
10.11	RMA	USL	a		L	1-3				7	9		8	10		2		4	1	3	5	6	11¹					
17.11	Royal Naval Depot	PSC1	h	considerable interest	L	1-4		p						p¹	p													p
21.11	Rifle Depot	USL	a		W	3-2					p³																	
24.11	RMLI	USL	h		W	6-3					9¹		8	10		3		6	1	2	5	4	8²	1	11²		7	
19.12	Naval Depot	USL	h		D	0-0		2			9	8			11	3					5	4	10			6		
05.01	Portsmouth Reserves	HSL	h		D	0-0					9	10	8			3		1	1	4	5	6	11					
12.01	Naval Depot	HSL	h		D	0-0					9		p						p	p	p							
16.01	20th Co RA	USL	a		D	0-0													p	p								
09.02	RMLI	USL	a		D	1-1							p¹															
23.02	Portsmouth Reserves	HSL	a	decent gate	W	2-1					p²								p	p²								
27.02	HMS Excellent	USL	a		W	5-1																						
02.03	Southampton Reserves	HSL	h		D	1-1				7	9	11	4			3			1	2	6	10	8¹					5
09.03	Naval Depot	HSL	a	goodly gathering	D	1-1												p¹		p								
13.03	RMA	USL	a	considerable interest	W	1-0				7	9	10				3		5	1	2	6	11	8					
20.03	RA Hilsea	USL	h		W	7-1				p¹	p³	p¹						1		p²		11						
30.03	Eastleigh	HSL	a		L	2-3																						
03.04	Rifle Depot	USL	h		W	2-0					p¹												p¹					
05.04	Southampton Reserves	HSL	a		D	1-1																						
20.04	Eastleigh	HSL	h		W																							

Notes: 05.01 Leach named in *Portsmouth Times* match report
20.03 score 8-1 in *Portsmouth Times*, no other scorer
03.04 score 3-0 in *Portsmouth Evening News*, no other scorer
07.11 Opponents given as 30th Co RA in *Hampshire Telegraph*
10.11 score 0-3 in *Portsmouth Times*
24.11 plus own goal (Beacon)

Royal Artillery – Honours List

1893/94   Army Cup **finalists** vs Depot RA (Gosport)
1894/95   Army Cup **winners** 2-0 vs Black Watch

1895/96   Hampshire Senior Cup **winners** 3-0 vs St Mary's Reserves
Amateur Cup **finalists**
Portsmouth Senior Cup **finalists**
Army Cup **semi-finalists**

1896/97   Army Cup **winners** 1-0 vs Lancashire Fusiliers
Portsmouth Senior Cup **winners** 5-0 vs Southsea Rovers
Hampshire Senior Cup **semi-finalists**
Hampshire Senior League **runners-up**

1897/98   Army Cup **finalists**
Southern League division two **champions**

1898/99   Army Cup **semi-finalists**
Amateur Cup **semi-finalists**

RA's successes in their five seasons as a first-class side amounted to:
FOUR national cup finals • **THREE** local cup finals • **THREE** further national semi-finals
ONE further local semi-final • as well as winning promotion from the Southern League's second division and becoming runners-up in the Hampshire Senior League.

The revived RA also became runners-up in the 1900/01 Hampshire Senior League in the side's only season following their demise at the hands of the Football Association.

Royal Artillery – Records

ARMY CUP

Win	8-1	1st Royal Welsh Fusiliers	R3	a	December 7, 1898
Defeat	1-3aet	1st South Lancashire Regiment	s-f		Villa Park, March 16, 1899
	0-2	2nd Gordon Highlanders	f		Aldershot, April 11, 1898

PORTSMOUTH SENIOR CUP

Win	15-0	Dublin Fusiliers	R1	h	November 14, 1896	*Consecutive*
	15-0	Army Service Corps	s-f		March 3, 1897	*fixture*
Defeat	0-4	Lancaster (King's Own) Regiment	R2	h	December 15, 1894	

HAMPSHIRE SENIOR CUP

Win	5-1aet	15th Co RA (Fareham)	R2	a	November 30, 1895
Defeat	0-3	15th Co SDRA (Fareham)	R1	a	November 24, 1894

AMATEUR CUP

Win	10-0	Clifton	R2q	h	November 2, 1895
	5-0	Maidenhead	R3	a	February 29, 1896
Defeat	0-1	Bishop Auckland	f		March 28, 1896
	2-3	Casuals	R2	a	February 13, 1897

HAMPSHIRE SENIOR LEAGUE

Win	(home)	8-0 Andover, September 26, 1896 *First game in competition.*
	(away)	6-0 Andover, March 6, 1897 *Return fixture*
Defeat	(away)	1-5 Eastleigh, September 4, 1897
	(home)	RA undefeated in **14 games**

SOUTHERN LEAGUE

Win	(home)	9-0 Maidenhead, SL2, December 11, 1897 *Consecutive and*
	(away)	5-0 Maidenhead, SL2, December 18, 1897 *return fixture*
Defeat	(home)	0-3 Bristol City, SL1, March 18, 1899
	(away)	0-8 Brighton Utd, SL1, September 24, 1898

ENGLISH CUP

Win	7-1	Eastleigh	prem 1	October 14, 1896
Defeat	1-4	Swindon T	prem 3	December 12, 1896
	0-3	Cowes	q2	October 20, 1898

SOUTHERN LEAGUE SEQUENCES

Most undefeated games	20	SL2	October 9, 1897 – March 30, 1898
Wins	17	SL2	November 27, 1897 – March 30, 1898
Winless	6	SL1	October 29, 1898 – December 17, 1898
Defeats	4	SL1	April 8, 1899 – April 29, 1899

HAMPSHIRE SENIOR LEAGUE SEQUENCES

Most undefeated games	12	September 26, 1896 – April 3, 1897
Wins	5	February 20, 1896 – April 3, 1897
Winless	2	April 24 and 28, 1896
	2	September 18 and 25, 1897
	2	April 2 and 16, 1898

ALL GAMES SEQUENCES

Most undefeated games		26 (out of 47) November 10, 1897 – March 30, 1898
		Southern League division two
	16	January 4 – March 17, 1896
		(before joining any leagues)
Consecutive wins	17	November 10, 1897 – March 30, 1898
Most winless games	4	April 2 – 16, 1897
	4	October 5 – 20, 1898
	4	April 8 – 29, 1899
Consecutive defeats	4	April 8 – 29, 1899
Most games in a season	47	1897/98
Fewest games in a season	22	1894/95
Most wins in a season	33	1897/98
Fewest wins in a season	12	1898/99
Most draws in a season	7	1895/96
Fewest draws in a season	3	1894/95
Most defeats in a season	19	1898/99
Fewest defeats in a season	3	1894/95

The 1900/01 season has been disregarded for this statistics section.

GOALS

Individual	league	4	Walsh	Andover	HSL	h	September 26, 1896
	cup	8	Tyre	HMS Vernon	PSCprem	h	October 31, 1896

ATTENDANCES

Cup	17,000 vs 2nd Gordon Highlanders in the Army Cup final, Aldershot, April 11, 1898
League	'Fully 8,000' vs Southampton, SL1, December 17, 1898
(home)	'No less than 7,000' vs Warmley, SL2, January 22, 1897
	Huge crowd vs Tottenham Hotspur, SL1, November 26, 1898